"In the 're-engineering age,' selling has not received the attention it deserves. Successful selling is an art, a science and a passion. Steve Sullivan has mastered it all, and his book is a great start at removing the mystery and applying solid common sense to successful selling while achieving it at lightening speed."
— Dana G. Mead
CEO, Tenneco

"The title fits the book. Steve operates at Mach 1 with his hair on fire. Move over Zig Ziglar, Sullivan and his book have gone public."
— Wayne H. Deitrich
President, Paper and Specialty Products,
Kimberly-Clark

"Steve Sullivan's book is the best piece of work I have read on the subject of selling. For those of us in the business of motivation and building closer relationships with clients and customers, it is a must read."
— Robert L. Pearson
Chairman,Lamalie Amrop International

"What a gold mine! Experience a lifetime of learning in a few hours of enthralling reading – humor, logic, and common sense!"
— C. Wesley Smith
Executive Vice President,
International Paper Company

"The experience of reading *Selling at Mach 1* is more aeronautical than literary. I felt like I was riding a rocket-ship to enlightenment."
— Randall Glendinning
COO, International Strategy Group

"*Selling at Mach 1* kept me rivetted to my reading chair for six straight hours. It has captured the essence of making the buyer feel important, inclined to do what the salesman wants and glad to do it. What else is left?"
— James Duncan
Vice President, Converting and Marketing,
Jefferson-Smurfit, Inc.

"If the customer is the final arbiter of value, then *Selling at Mach 1* delivers a highly creative, comprehensive, and straightforward approach to let the buyers and sellers of goods and services become business partners for life."
— James M. Curran
Division Director, IBM

"I've purchased my last book on selling. In short *Selling at Mach 1* is as close to being a masterpiece as anything I've ever read on the subject."
— O. William Battalia
Chairman, Battalia Winston International

"Steve Sullivan leaves no stone unturned in his approach of putting the customer first, and what he uncovers in his search for excellence will help make you a selling superstar."
— Paul Stecko
CEO, Packaging Corporation of America

"The bible on selling is now in print."
— Stephen Hitchcock
President, Matrix International

"Forget the economic bottom line, there are more important things. *Selling at Mach 1* is a recipe for success in life. It will be a mandatory read for my children."
— Mignette Hollyman
Mother

▲

SELLING
AT
MACH 1

▲

SELLING
AT
MACH 1

Motivational Acceleration

▲

Steven D. Sullivan

A Motivational Resources Book

A Motivational Resources Book,
Motivational Resources,
54 Danbury Road, Suit 308,
Ridgefield, Connecticut 06877
in association with Karl Wendt, Ltd.
Cologne, Germany

Editor and Advisor, Amy J. Pecora

Book Cover Design by Patti Britton,
Britton Designs, Sonoma, California
Chapter Illustrations by Maria Lauricella,
New York, New York

10 9 8 7 6 5 4 3 2 1

ISBN: 0–9641053–0–6

To purchase additional copies,
please write or call:
Motivational Resources
54 Danbury Road, Suite 308
Ridgefield, Connecticut 06877
(203) 438–5952

To Lloyd and Ruth
Parents don't get any more supportive!

To Elizabeth and Erin
There is no greater joy than having
you as my daughters.

▲

Selling At Mach 1

On October 14, 1947, 8 miles above the
Mojave Desert, General Chuck Yeager,
a bonafied American hero, flew the
experimental X-1 in excess
of the speed of sound -
Mach 1.

CONTENTS

FORWARD

Drawing on over 20 years of exceptional success as a salesman, marketeer, and senior manager, Steve Sullivan lays out a foolproof approach to becoming a sales superstar in *Selling at Mach 1*. If you've never been exposed to his concepts on selling, fasten your safety belt and get ready for the literary self-help ride of your life.

Selling involves getting others to give you what you want and I'm convinced no one understands the process better than Sullivan. I've watched his success over the past fifteen years and I'm surprised by the title. I always thought he sold at Mach 3 !

Whether he was closing a sale, motivating his team, or energizing an organization, the results came so quickly it often seemed like magic. Now that I've read *Selling at Mach 1*, I know it wasn't.

The concepts, terminology, and applicability of Motivational Acceleration are so fundamentally sound and easy to apply, when you've finished the book your ability to sell will take a quantum leap forward. Nothing I've ever read on the subject so accurately diagnoses and dissects the sales transaction from initial encounter to order placement.

Delivered in a no-nonsense anecdotal style, *Selling at Mach 1* clears the senses, tickles the funny bone, and gives you a formula for success that could take you into the Salesman's Hall of Fame.

This is an action book written by a former Army Ranger who knows how to get things done. The journey from start to finish occurs at breakneck speed. Being satisfied is not in Sullivan's repertoire. Winning is the goal, and that is what he offers the reader, the opportunity to take it all.

William Pollert
Senior Vice President
Triarc Companies Inc.

*I don't know what your destiny will be,
but one thing I know, the only ones among
you who will be really happy are those who
have sought and found how to serve.*

Albert Schweitzer

PROLOGUE

This book is about selling, pure and simple. It started out as a 450-page dissertation on the subject, but when I realized it wouldn't be sold by the pound, I edited out everything that was meaningless and the pages you have remaining say as much about selling as needs to be said.

The thoughts presented are my own. I'm not sure any of them are original! I've read the books, I know all the buzzwords, and I'm aware that there are countless ways to open and close a sale. Sales expertise is everywhere and that's why I'm confused.

Given the abundance of material that is available, it's perplexing that so many people can't sell. The process escapes them. Part of it can be blamed on marketing, a basic tenet of which involves one's ability to differentiate oneself.

If you want to sell a book, a sales manual, or a sales training program, your information needs to look different than what's already in print. Terminology becomes important. How many different ways can you say, "Ask for the order."

I have no idea how much has been written on the subject; I suspect too much. It all starts to run together. These thoughts presented, under the heading of Motivational Acceleration, are my attempt to clear the air and to focus on what is absolutely fundamental in any sales situation. Don't let the title scare you. I know that when you say the two words together, "Motivational Acceleration," it sounds like something out of a think tank. It's not! Think tanks scare me. There is too much thinking going on.

Whatever success I've achieved has come about through practical application and therefore I discount most theories until they have been proven through Action. I tell you this because I want you to understand what you are about to read is much more than one man's thoughts on the subject of selling.

I'm a product of what I've been taught, observed, and experienced. I take no credit for originality because everything I present has come from others. I am nothing more than a facilitator who has synthesized a lifetime of experience into a document of "Straight Talk" on Selling. Selling at Mach 1 is not theory. It is a recipe for success that, if implemented, will make you a superior salesman.

Now, before we go any further, let's come to an understanding. When I use the word salesman, I'm doing so in a gender-free capacity. Salesman as in mankind. There are salesmen and saleswomen.

Salesmen act upon buyers. The Buyer, in whatever position they occupy – boss, prospective date, builder, maitre d', customer, spouse, bartender, or service agent, have the ability to give something to the seller. It could be time, money, effort, or consideration. The buyer is your Target of Opportunity.

The Salesman on the other hand, is an offensive agent. He or she initiates the action and is desirous of having the Buyer make a move that is in his or her best interest. Are there variations on this theme? Absolutely! But without getting into semantics, or exploring every aspect of buyer/seller relationships, I think this simple explanation will get us started.

For a perfect sales situation to exist, both parties' interests need to be equally served. But this isn't a perfect world and this book isn't about fairness. It's about motivating another individual to give you what you want, in your professional life, and in your personal life. It seems reasonable to me, the more accelerated the pace at which you achieve your goals, the more you will accomplish. Motivational Acceleration is about a lot of things, none of which is more important than compressing the time it takes to make things happen.

AN OBSERVATION

It's only a matter of time until youthful idealism passes, and you start to realize that success in life is not a given. If you are going to make an impact, there is a window of opportunity in which to do it. Whatever you are going to achieve will have to happen within defined time boundaries. Certainly, the spectrum of accomplishment will vary between individuals. Life span, energy level, or other determinants broaden or lessen it, but recognize this. Your productive years will come to an end.

Given that fact, it's been interesting to observe at what stage in a person's existence, if at all, they get turned on, take charge and try to accomplish something. With many people, it doesn't happen until they are a long way into life's journey. Alexander the Great must have known he would die at 32. If he wanted to conquer the world he needed to do it quickly. History is populated by individuals whose ignition spark came at an early age. We all enjoy the benefits of their effort and accomplishment.

Others never live up to their potential. Their life is characterized by one failure after another, and they don't understand why. On the surface they appear to have as much going for them as anyone else, but nothing of any consequence ever happens. Success in most things escapes them. Little did they know the slightest behavioral modification would have made all the difference.

If you chronicled their life, the foundation for mediocrity or failure was built early on. In adolescence, things came easy. Mom and Dad provided. The more that was provided in the formative years, the greater the optimism was that things will always be that way. Few young people understand that when the providers are gone, they will have to provide for themselves. From youth, they carry with them a naive belief that things will proceed upward because they exist. A convoluted manifest destiny or divine intervention will govern what happens. Their future success is secure, and nothing much is required. A cornucopia of rewarding experiences is waiting to be harvested, just take your pick.

Unfortunately, as time marches inexorably forward, the muted tones of a childhood fantasy take on a sharper edge. The image crystallizes. There is no Porsche in the driveway! The house on the hill looks surprisingly like a two-bedroom apartment! You haven't had a promotion in years! It's time for a wake up call.

Now if I were a betting man, I'd wager you're convinced that maybe you don't know everything there is about selling. You wouldn't have purchased this book if you weren't looking for self-improvement. But I'd also bet that you harbor a view that there is plenty of time to get started, that the important sales of your life are at some distant juncture. I suggest that the quicker you get going the better you will do.

I say that because the greatest opportunity you may ever encounter might present itself tomorrow. Not knowing how to close the sale could prove costly. When I think about the opportunities and successes I've had, many seemed to sprout from something unexpected. They materialized quickly, and if anything were to be made of them, time was of the essence. If you can't get the fish to bite, there is no potential for bringing it in.

When I was younger, I viewed my future and how it would progress in stages. I thought that there would be a clear delineation between when one part ended and the next began. I saw my life's journey as Robert Frost might have seen it in his famous poem, The Road Not Taken. That road meanders along until it splits in the woods and then you take one fork or another. I envisioned, that as I progressed, there would be three or four times where I would have to make The Choice. There was plenty of time to prepare.

The fact is the road splits hundreds of times in your life. There will be a myriad of individual encounters with each one having the potential to provide something that moves you in a different, more rewarding and exciting direction. In a nutshell, it is other people who will determine where you end up. They will provide you with your opportunities.

Acceptance, inclusion, reward, recognition, and promotion rests in the minds of others. How you influence their willingness to support your efforts is up to you. You are in control, but until you understand what a critical impact your actions have on another individual's view of you, you will never achieve as much as you could.

INTRODUCTION

Do you spend a lot of time thinking about success? I do. Most people do. I'm constantly evaluating my situation in relationship to where I thought I would be, where I want to be. I'll bet you do the same thing, and in doing so, you can't help but compare yourself to others. It is a relative world we live in. There will always be individuals who accomplish less and people who accomplish more. What should be noted is, often times, there is very little correlation between hard work-success, intelligence-success, and overall ability-success. Life is unfair.

How did these people: business executives, generals, actors, educators, doctors, lawyers, scientists, entrepreneurs, politicians and a host of others get where they are? In an earlier century we would have assumed that they were tapped for greatness because they were superior. A hundred years ago, the communication age was a Jules Verne fantasy, not present day reality. Information moved slowly, if at all. You could blunder and no one knew. You might be a fool and only an intimate circle of associates was aware of it. Today's environment is quite different. Information is delivered almost instantaneously.

Through satellite dishes, cable, network programming, VCR's and radio, the circus has come to our living room. We are painfully aware of the shortcomings of some of those individuals whom we've placed on a pedestal. But let's stop right here!

This book isn't about our ability to survive with dummies minding the store. It's about success. Success achieved through selling.

Everywhere you look there are people who have achieved greater financial gain, job satisfaction and emotional nourishment than yourself. Seemingly, they are more successful, and success in my mind is a life characterized by a higher level of participation, accomplishment, and reinforcement. Who doesn't want that? Having meaningful relationships with others is important. With the world population approaching six billion, it's quite unlikely you'll be able to escape interpersonal interaction, and therein lies a reason to finish *Selling at Mach 1*. When you have, you will better understand the sales process and how to successfully adapt it to your own circumstances. You will be better prepared to achieve things through people.

Let's briefly get back to those individuals who we know are no better than us, but for some reason have accomplished more. If we examined ten cases of success and juxtaposed one against another, we would see tremendous variability in how that success came about. We would see differences in physical appearance, intelligence, sense of urgency, effort, and much more. Is there a common denominator? Absolutely!!! Their ability to sell.

Now I can see your mind working, "That's them, what about me?". What about you? It's time you recognized it. You are a Salesman.

Don't be frightened, you're in good company. Eleanor Roosevelt – First Lady – Salesman, Billy Graham – Evangelist – Salesman, Norman Schwartzkopf – General – Salesman, Abraham Lincoln – President – Salesman. Occupation, avocation, association, it doesn't matter. Everyone is a Salesman! You may not have it on your business card, but I guarantee you a majority of your life will be spent selling. The sooner you understand that the better off you will be.

We might as well start with a definition. That's easier said than done. People have been selling for as long as there have been people. It is the oldest profession. The act of selling has always been with us and I suppose it always will. I'm not sure there is one optimum definition for selling, and there probably shouldn't be. If you ask any group of people to define selling you would get a diverse set of answers. Whatever their response, it is a result of their individual exposure to the sales process. It's easy to understand why selling is viewed so differently.

If everyone is a seller, then the act of selling is a ubiquitous occurrence. We see it everywhere. We've seen it our entire life. From our initial entry into the cognitive world, we have been sold. While you were sitting in a high chair, your mother tried to sell you on the proposition that cold mashed carrots were good for you. What was her approach? Did you buy it or did you reject the sale? Did you eat those carrots or spit them out?

A sales transaction was taking place, and who would have guessed. It's been that way as long as you've been alive. You are constantly being sold, and you are continually selling. You, like a lot of people, may not label it "selling," but it is. Call it what you want, here's a fact. If you are trying to influence another person to do something, you are selling. If you succeed more than you fail, you probably have an understanding of the process and if the reverse is true, don't worry, help is on the way. But, before you can get help you have to accept what you are. Not the totality of your being, but an aspect of your behavior.

Selling is a human behavior manifesting itself in some form. If it makes you happier to call it your style, go ahead. As long as you understand your style influences others. No sales transaction has ever taken place unless at least one other person was involved. Now it seems logical to me that if our actions impact others, we would want to behave in such a way that the impression we make on them is favorable.

A "normal" person is not knowingly looking to make unfavorable impressions. If they do, it usually is because of ignorance. They weren't aware of the signals they were sending or they were oblivious to the damage their actions caused. The interaction was brief but the negative impact was long-lasting. I guess leaving negative impressions won't hurt you if you live in a vacuum, but the fact is you don't. What others think of you is important! How they feel about you most often determines how they react to you. Their response, good, bad or indifferent affects you - financially and emotionally.

I'm going to make the assumption now that you have accepted the fact that you are a salesman. If I don't, I can't continue, because everything that follows has to do with Selling. I get the feeling you still aren't sure.

THE FEAR OF BEING LABELED...
A SALESMAN

What is it about the words "salesman," and "saleswoman," that turns so many people off? Past experience, perception, ignorance? Probably a combination of all those things and more! In the minds of many, the selling process has always had negative connotations...manipulation, deceit, and dishonesty. Many people have had a hard time separating the dynamics of selling from the salesman.

There is no question salesmen have abused their customers since the act of selling began. It's perfectly understandable why so many individuals have trouble accepting the concept of being a salesman. It must have something to do with guilt by association. Even sales professionals who have successfully performed the duties, whose paycheck comes from selling, shy away from the label. They would rather be called marketing representatives, account executives, and district managers. You would think Pontius Pilate had been Vice President of Sales for Rome. He wasn't, and being labeled a salesman is something you should take pride in. Selling involves getting results. It takes communication skills, flexibility, hard work, knowledge, creativity and a strong ego. Rejection is part of the game, and selling involves a lot of rejection. Less, when you know what you are doing. Insecure people have a tough time. In the selling profession, measurement is easy. Success is very objective. Did you get the order or not? Was your proposal accepted or were you turned down?

In business or in personal relationships, nothing happens until a sale is made or until another individual says, "yes". It is the catalyst for future activity. Most successful people will tell you, no matter what level of recognition and accomplishment they have achieved, they still sell. No, don't be afraid of being called a salesman...Embrace it!

Think people.

THE BASICS

There is only one success – to be able to
spend your own life in your own way.
— *Christopher Morley*

Think about the number of people you encounter in a day. How many individuals do you interface with in the course of living a typical day: ten, twenty, a hundred? Certainly the answer varies, but my guess is, you would be surprised by the number if you ever totaled it.

The fact is people are everywhere! We may be able to get away from them on a trek to Katmandu, but in our regular day-to-day living there is no escape.

Rational thought would dictate in those areas where we must interact with another human being, we would want that encounter to be as pleasant as possible. In many cases we want more than just pleasantness. We want something from them. Productivity!

I might be a little demanding, but I'll bet I'm not asking for any more than you. The fact is, all things are possible. Whether you achieve what you want in life is up to you, but recognize your fate is not in your hands, it's in the hands of others.

What Do The Smart Guys Say

There are a number of experts on the subject of selling that would tell you no sale will be made unless the buyer, in whatever form they exist, perceives that you are fulfilling a need. I agree, but let's explore that concept a bit further. The mind is not a calculator. The empirical solutions needed to solve a math problem are seldom appropriate in the decision making process when trying to overcome a people problem. It's been proven that the majority of all decisions are emotional in nature. People act or react in accordance with how they feel about something.

It's estimated that up to 80% of all decisions are made by the right side of the brain, the emotional side. Did you really need those 20 boxes of Girl Scouts cookies? Take the 1992 presidential election. There was no question about some of the measures George Bush needed to take to increase his chances of retaining the presidency. It was obvious he had to fire a number of his key advisors who had not performed. Why didn't he? I suspect from what I've read about President Bush, he is intensely loyal to his subordinates. He would rather risk the loss of a position he held dear than violate a principle of his psychological makeup. He lost his job. They still lost theirs. An emotional decision that was clearly not in his best interest, but it was still made.

Nobody but a fool would try to make the case that satisfying needs isn't important in the selling process. Any successful salesman must be able to identify what the buyer needs. Unfortunately, that's just part of the game. It's the price of admission. It will get you in the ballpark but when you walk on to the field you'll find a number of other players wanting to take your position. Their success is incumbent upon "doing you in."

I've encountered a number of salesmen over the years that naively believed once they identified a customer's need and had a satisfactory solution, the order was theirs. They were mistaken. They didn't realize that need satisfaction was within the capability of any of their viable competitors.

Finding out what a customer needs oftentimes is no more difficult than phrasing the question, "What do you need?" The customer will usually tell you. Now what happens is you, along with a number of competitors, has that information and the ability to perform. Who gets the order?

My experience indicates it is the salesman who exerts the most influence over the customer. The order is his or hers based upon factors that had nothing to do with need. Satisfying needs will help you sell but if you want to close at Mach 1, you'll have to do more.

Many decisions are devoid of logic or rationality. Understanding the dynamics of a buyer's decision making process is what Motivational Acceleration is about. In its most complex form, it is nothing more than applying fundamental behavioral science principles to personal relationships to develop them rapidly.

It's a kind of chemical engineering. Do you remember chemistry lab? Nitrogen and calcium when combined elicited no reaction. When you exposed iron to oxygen, you detected something was happening, but the reaction was slow. You had to wait awhile. What happened when water met potassium? You had a kind of spontaneous combustion. The second they encountered each other...Bingo...you had something.

The human being is a little more complex, and our ability to determine what exactly will happen when two personalities meet is less certain. There are lots of different ways electricity moves through brain matter. Chemistry is an exact science. Psychology is not. It is true, in our association with other people, their reaction to our actions is less manageable. It comes with how synapses fire. But by understanding some critical components of the relationship building process, we certainly can do much better in determining outcomes.

Motivational Acceleration requires you to be

smart. Not intellectually smart, operationally smart. It demands almost a religious belief that others are the key to your success and happiness in life. If those that surround you are unhappy with you, I can guarantee you (100% probability), you will be unhappy, unproductive, and unfulfilled.

PLEASE DON'T PISTOL–WHIP ME, MISTER

I've worked in New York City for ten years now and have experienced much of what the Big Apple has to offer with one exception. I've never been mugged. I know a lot of people who have though, and having heard countless stories about what transpires, I'm of the opinion there is a school for muggers somewhere on West 61st Street.

Their modus operandi never changes. The attack is swift, aggressive, and highly impersonal. Muggers don't preplan. They go after targets of opportunity. It is always a one-sided affair. The mugger initiates the action, dominates the conversation, and has no concept of quid pro quo.

As I'm writing this, I'm starting to experience déjà vu. I have been mugged! The encounter was identical. The only difference was the mugger didn't carry a gun. He carried a sample bag of encyclopedias. His MO was the same. He approached quickly, did all the talking, and took my money. My reaction was no different than any muggee. I felt violated and used.

Do you think my analogy is a little far-fetched? I

wish it were. Unfortunately there are many parallels between a street criminal and a bad salesman.

❶ They are interested in self-gratification.

❷ They're abusive.

❸ They don't understand the consequences of their actions.

❹ Their focus is short term.

❺ It's only a matter of time before they get caught.

We could go on but I think you get the picture.

In contrast, Motivationally Accelerated selling is the exact opposite of what has just been described.

❶ Accelerators focus on others.

❷ They are supportive.

❸ They are well aware of the impact of their behavior.

❹ Their perspective is long term.

❺ Their success is never ending.

Now, having said all this, I'm continually amazed at how negatively human beings relate to other human beings. It's bad enough if you will never see the individual again, but it takes on overtones of monumental stupidity if you want to influence another individual to help you succeed, and then violate the basic tenets of good behavior.

Look around you. I'm not sure what is causing it but there are a lot of people walking around with attitude problems. Curt, caustic, selfish, and inconsiderate are just a few of the adjectives that describe their actions. Is it any wonder why they may not be achieving what they want from others. Do they think success comes in a vacuum? Accelerated thinking may not change your attitude about others, but it will enlighten you to the consequences of your behavior.

Are you thoughtful, kind, courteous, obedient, honest, and trustworthy in your relationships with others? It sounds like the Boy Scouts creed. Do you treat people like you would want to be treated? Holy cow, the Golden Rule! You see, when we sell we are interacting with another person who reacts to stimuli much the same way we do. They try to avoid people and situations that engender discomfort. Normal people will gravitate to those they like and resist those they don't like.

THE COLD, HARD FACTS

We live in a world of limited resources. Each of us has only so much time, money, and energy, and because of that we have to make choices! People, whom you are trying to sell, have to make choices also. Not everyone can have The Order. As with most things in life, there are winners and losers. The winners are usually those individuals who get noticed. The losers live in the shadows. They do what everyone else is doing. Their life is characterized by a never-ending series of Non-Events. They give nothing above the ordinary, and therefore get nothing in return.

THE NON-EVENT

In order to facilitate your understanding of the sales process, let's identify some terms that I think accurately express what is going on in any inter-personal relationship. Right from the start, the moment you encounter another person, you are making an impression on them; physical appear-ance, enthusiasm, and communication all play a part. They internalize what they see and hear, and start to form an opinion about you. If you are your basic average person in all these areas, the impres-sion you make on them will be negligible. Nothing much happens and you have, what from this point forward will be referred to as, a Non-Event.

Non-Events exist for only one reason: The indi-vidual doing the selling chooses not to put forth the effort to make the interpersonal interaction memorable.

The majority of all interpersonal interactions are Non-Events. Of the 35 people you interfaced with yesterday, how many of them were memorable? If you've taken any sales training courses, you have been taught that a critical component of selling is differentiating yourself from the competition. It's true.

If you believe it, then recognize that being aver-age does not set you apart. Most people are average. It's not an indictment, it's a fact. If everyone were outstanding, then outstanding would become average. The majority of us don't fall into that category, but that doesn't mean we can't stand out, and standing out is necessary if you are going to make a positive impression on your customer.

ACCELERATION

Forget the Non-Event, let's create events through Acceleration. Acceleration is nothing more than focusing your efforts in areas that turn people on, get them excited, and make them want to have a relationship with you.

Back to chemistry. If you do a quick review of your recent past with regard to relationships, I'm sure you can recount an experience where the emotional bonding came very quickly. Everything seemed to work. The other person was genuinely interested in what you were presenting and accepted it without resistance. Why? Did you know what you were doing, or was the human chemistry, by accident, just right? Now reflect back on an encounter where things weren't quite so easy. Communication was strained. Everything was debated, and when the interpersonal interlude was over, you didn't feel very good about it. What happened?

Not knowing either party or the circumstances, I wouldn't venture a guess. I will tell you in the first situation, you were Accelerating, and in the second, you were Decelerating. In one case a variety of elements were presented that bonded harmoniously and the psychological union came rapidly... Acceleration. The sale was made. In the other situation, the wrong elements were injected and the relationship deteriorated...Deceleration. No Sale! Now if selling was chemistry, it would be easy to determine what is needed to produce specific results.

Through trial and error, virtually every conceivable combination of elements has been tested and their reactions recorded. One part potassium with one part water and you know the outcome. Unfortunately, the brain is not a table of elements. Just ask Sigmund Freud.

Take one part rudeness, one part dishonesty, a little arrogance and what will happen? Freud isn't sure. He would tell you the relationship is heading south, but whether it's by bicycle, train, or Lear jet, he has no way of knowing. There are too many variables. How will it finally end? A "Dear John" letter, a locked door, or banishment. Sigmund can only speculate, and if one of the world's foremost authorities on human behavior can't accurately predict the specific impact of one individual's actions on another, does it really matter how you behave? The answer is obvious. Of course, it does!

I firmly believe salesmen Decelerate with customers because of the absence of empirical data showing quantifiable evidence that behavior, good or bad, has a dramatic effect. The customer may not immediately act on their feelings, but over time, the cumulative effect of what the salesman does for them, with them, or to them will determine the quality of their relationship and ultimately, its success.

Certainly the customer is partly responsible for the treatment they receive. Good communication is characterized by an open expression of how each party feels. If the customer was unhappy with some aspect of how they were being treated, and made the salesman aware of it, ("I don't like your rudeness and I'm going to penalize you for it") I suspect the salesman would adjust his behavior immediately. Unfortunately, for the salesman, feelings often aren't expressed until irreparable damage has been done.

Now the scramble is on, and the salesman has to work four times as hard just to get back to a position where the customer might consider him as a resource. Wouldn't it have been easier to do things the right way up front? It would if you knew what to do and what not to do. Obviously, you would want to do things that score points with your customer, and refrain from those activities that lose you points. Let's look at a buyer/seller interpersonal relationship model:

Spectrum of Influence

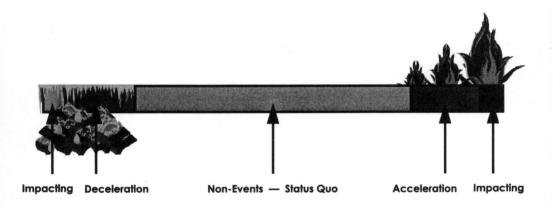

Impacting Deceleration   Non-Events — Status Quo   Acceleration Impacting

In any interpersonal relationship, how one individual relates to another is in large part a result of the degree of influence that exists between them. Influence is a necessity in getting another individual to act on something. In normal relationships, influence is gained over an extended period of time.

It evolves. In Motivationally Accelerated relationships, it materializes.

Earlier, we said it was difficult to quantify behavior because of all the variables that come into play when two personalities interact. Difficult? Yes. Impossible? No! In order for you to better evaluate where you are in a relationship, being able to keep score is important. We live in a society where scoring determines success or failure. In most cases, the higher the score, the better the performance. Obviously golf is an exception, and maybe that's why it's so frustrating. We have been conditioned to score and are rewarded for it. Forget golf. Our Motivationally Accelerated program will use a standard of measurement that encourages big numbers.

In some ways, Motivational Acceleration is like playing pinball. Think of your customer as the playing surface and yourself as the pinball. If you are just rolling around and making no contact, there is no score. In certain areas, your contact scores points. In other areas, characterized as danger zones, if you encounter them you lose points and your turn. The object is to maneuver in such a way that you are scoring points while staying out of danger zones. If you are successful, at some point, you will score enough to earn a reward.

In selling, the dynamics are pretty much the

same. The object is to score with the customer, and when you have achieved an acceptable number of points, a reward will follow. How much is needed? Good question. I have no idea. I will tell you, it will vary with every customer you have. There is no set number. There are just too many variables. History, personality, performance, internal and external influences, and a host of other factors will dictate when and how you score. They will also determine the time frame that governs your ascent from a Non-Event to supplier of choice. That climb can be long and arduous or short and exhilarating. As with any journey, what happens along the way is in large part a result of your preparation up front. In the world of selling, it all starts with knowledge.

NOTES

To the embassy, please.

ALL-STATE VS. SECRETARY OF STATE

Knowledge is the only instrument
of production that is not subject
to diminishing returns.
— J.M. Clark

In 1938, when George Washington High School played their cross-town rival in football, if you asked who was playing linebacker for George Washington, the answer would not have been Henry Kissinger. If you scanned the stadium to see who was cheering for the home team, in all probability Henry's face would not have been present. It wasn't that Henry didn't have an interest in sports, it just took a back seat to more important activities.

He understood whatever athletic prowess he achieved in his youth would diminish with age. He was interested in investing his energy in something that would grow stronger with time...knowledge.

Henry didn't look like Cary Grant, and some say he moved like a handcuffed hippopotamus, but he was smart enough to know that none of that mattered. Being able to play on the world stage was a function of smarts, not physical capability. All-State athletes are forgotten after the senior prom, while secretaries of state go into the history books.

Stupid went out with dinosaurs, dumb has never been in, and idiocy will get you a job as an assistant janitor. The world is being run by "Brain Power," not muscle power. Linebackers work for nerds and isn't that a wonderfully just circumstance. It doesn't matter that genetics slam-dunked you when it came to appearance, because in the long run what you know always wins out over how you look. You can forgive your high school associates who didn't invite you to join their fraternity or sorority by inviting them to your inaugural ball.

THERE IS NO SUBSTITUTE FOR KNOWLEDGE!

From the moment you walk through a customer's door, you are being evaluated and compared. Evaluated on what you bring to the relationship, as well as compared to your competition, past and present.

Failure on your part to grasp the essentials of the

business relationship relegates you to second-class citizenship. Any decision maker who runs a successful enterprise expects the salesman who gets a disproportionate share of their business to be a major contributor in the area of intelligence. Timely, accurate information is the price of admission.

For those of you who have an empirical bent, let me express it more mathematically: C_2FKC_4. A simple formula that states your **Competence** and **Confidence** as a salesman is a **Function** of your **Knowledge** of the **Customer**, **Competitor**, **Company**, and your **Capabilities**.

Only by having knowledge will you be able to chart a course that keeps you off the reefs, at full sail, in open water. Knowing what is important to your customers, allows you to expend effort in only those areas that favorably impact them. Trial and error becomes trial and success. Success builds a confidence that mandates further experimentation. Rejection is no longer feared. You now want more speed. You need a bigger boat and larger sails.

Slow down! We don't want you to capsize.

Remember what I said about knowledge. Virtually anyone can acquire it. The reality is that of the ten individuals you may be in competition with, at least two are as knowledgeable in key areas as yourself. Your challenge is to break away from the pack by establishing a perception of superior intellect. Let's do a little analysis on the subject of intelligence. If your IQ was 90 or 165 and you said nothing, no one would know. Only through expressions of thought will another person start to form opinions about your ability to think.

An interesting dynamic of silence is, when it exists, individuals have time to contemplate why it exists. Is there an underlying reason? Are they not speaking because they are too busy contemplating the secrets of the universe, or are they so smart they can't communicate at lower levels?

Over the years individuals have been identified to me as genius, and as I got to know them nothing was farther from the truth. They spoke very little because they had difficulty getting their brain out of first gear. They did understand the process of creating an image about superior intellect by keeping their mouths closed. Periodically, when the forum was right, they would drop a "pearl of wisdom," a quote from Shakespeare, how many pounds of thrust it took to launch a satellite, or the year the cotton gin was invented, and shut up. The information was insignificant enough that no one else knew it. Gosh, they're smart. Wrong! They read it that morning in the newspaper.

It's a fact that people want to be around others of equal or superior intelligence and will gravitate to them. As an Accelerator, you want to be an intellectual magnet. It's important you learn as much as you can about as many things as you can when it relates to your customer.

Certainly time is a factor, and it will take time to build your foundation of knowledge. In the interim though, there is nothing that prevents you from influencing a perception of being knowledgeable. Acquire thirty or forty intellectual jewels that you can deposit when the time is right. Make sure they are of interest to your customer. If they are into square dancing, and you just happen to drop the year that square dancing started, it shows knowledge in an area that is meaningful to them. Five points. Deliver a quote from someone they respect. Five points. Send them an article about overcoming a problem they have. Five points.

Another attribute of knowledge is that it's portable. You carry it with you. It's not in the trunk of your car. It's between your ears. You never know when or where an opportunity will present itself. Having the Library of Congress sitting on your shoulders saves a lot of gas and time.

WHEN PHYSICAL PROWESS GOES BYE-BYE

The smartest individual I've met in American industry is Dana Mead, president of Tenneco, a $13 billion conglomerate. He was once a three-sport, all-state athlete from Illinois, but that was long ago and far away. The seventy-eight thousand people that depend on him for their livelihood don't care how fast he can run the 40-yard dash. They do care how his mind works.

As a Ph.D. from MIT, Dana certainly has the ability to think through any issue. He could wax for hours on the stress factors encountered by the rivets that hold the wings on the space shuttle. But, because he has to periodically wear his Motivational Acceleration selling cap, he recognizes the need to stay current. Customers want information that is timely and event specific. It has to be relative. Stress factors are a perfect substitute for sleeping pills.

There are those that think he is the brightest guy in corporate America. He could be, but I will tell you many of the tidbits of information he leaves with his customers were not extracted from his cerebrum. He researched them shortly before the encounter. I told you he was an Accelerator. If he's invited by a customer to fish for salmon in Alaska, he buys a book on everything you ever wanted to know about Alaska and salmon fishing.

When you pull your first big fish from the river, Dana will explain to you the chemical composition of its scales, and why the river's temperature at 63 degrees was perfect for salmon activity and your choice of fly. In the course of a three-day outing, you will learn more than you did in college. The event will come to an end, and you will tell your friends he is the smartest guy in the universe.

The three-hour investment in time Dana made to gather that information will soon be rewarded. Everyone wants to do business with a knowledgeable person. If he knew that much about how far a salmon can see in turgid rapids, how much does he know about important things? The question is obviously rhetorical. I've spent years around him, and his phone never stops ringing.

Success in business starts with access to the person you want to sell. Whether they view you as a resource or an albatross is your call. The tools needed to influence the correct perception are everywhere. Use them!

You don't need forty different articles on something intellectually stimulating. Visit your local Kinko's copy center. You'll find, as you help your customers overcome their challenges through knowledge, your phone will never stop ringing.

It's all in your perspective.

MOTIVATIONAL ACCELERATION:
A Road Map

It takes less time to do a thing right than
to explain why you did it wrong.
— Henry Wadsworth Longfellow

Let's start with a definition.

Motivational Acceleration:

A calculated series of actions that allows you to benchmark the quality of your customer relationships and then implement a program that dramatically improves them at an accelerated pace.

If I were to analyze what I have just defined as Motivational Acceleration, I'd say it comes across as a bit abstruse. It's supposed to, only because we are still involved in framing the concept. Form has to precede substance. Think of Motivational Acceleration as the exterior of a house. The house does not become a home until a lot of meaningful ingredients are placed within it. There have been many salesmen who have been taught the process of selling, been given the framework on how to sell but never understood that their approach had virtually no substance.

They were Selling Automatons, glorious in their ability to perform a variety of tasks on time within prescribed limits, but their impact was negligible. They never connected with their customer. They looked the part, but for everything they did right, they countered it with ten actions that were wrong. Why? They didn't know any better. Somewhere they were taught or developed an illusion that action, in and of itself, has worth. If you expend so much energy, success is bound to follow.

SPARE THE HORSES!

The premise of Accelerated Thinking dictates you engage only in actions that positively impact the customer. No wasted effort allowed. You save your energy for those activities that get results. There are plenty of analogies to illustrate this point in sports, politics, business, etc.

In that I spent the first six years of my working career as a soldier, I'll use a militaristic example. I'm sure you remember the Vietnam War. If you weren't directly involved, I'll assume you have at least some knowledge as to what transpired. In the final stages, a strategic decision was made to "Bomb North Vietnam into oblivion." Day after day, B-52s dropped thousands of tons of bombs indiscriminately across the northern tier of Vietnam with limited results. If you calculated the total expense of this bombing activity, and juxtaposed it against the number of enemy soldiers killed, the cost per kill would be in the millions of dollars.

The plan meant throwing everything we had at them in hopes there would be positive outcome. It failed! Two decades later technological advances in weaponry allowed the Air Force to take a different approach in the Iraqi showdown. You didn't need to drop a hundred bombs at a target, knowing only three might hit, when you could drop one "Smart Bomb" and feel assured the job was done.

In the sniper units in infantry battalions, there is a saying, "One shot, one kill." It's pretty self-explanatory. If you carry the qualification, Sniper, with one pull of the trigger you achieve the desired result...one dead. The resources expended are minimal. The cost/benefit ratio is low.

Now let's extricate ourselves from this talk of death. We're not killers. We're salesmen. But, our job is no less life threatening. A different kind of fatality, but death none the less. Without salesmen doing their jobs effectively, an organization will surely meet its demise.

Motivational Acceleration prevents that from

happening, and it does so through a series of steps that energize the relationship. We calculate because we need to understand the situation. We benchmark so we can measure where we are in the relationship. We Accelerate because the quicker we move ahead, the more we can accomplish. Let's get specific.

In any sales situation some kind of relationship exists. Its intensity runs the gamut from very positive (lots of success), to very negative (no success). The strength of the relationship is a product of how the individuals feel about each other, and those feelings are not born through immaculate conception. They exist as a result of behavior.

To Accelerate a relationship, it is imperative your actions create a positive perception a majority of the time. Whether you call it common courtesy, etiquette, civility, or good manners, there is no shortage of information on the subject of how to relate to others.

Although we live in an age where the boundaries of acceptable behavior have been stretched, I would suggest they have not been broken. As a matter of fact, in customer relationships, the parameters are pretty tight. They like you to say please and thank you. Your customer needs to have some criteria by which to evaluate and measure you. If you were the only individual trying to sell them, you might be able to get away with a periodic lapse in performance. The reality is, you are just one of many solicitors looking for an order. It's called competition.

You are not only graded on what you are doing, in an absolute sense, you are being evaluated in relation to others.

If you do something the customer doesn't agree with, you drop a notch in their eyes. If your competitor performs in an acceptable manner in that area, they move up a notch. Get the picture? It's a double whammy, but you can reverse who gets whacked.

We stated earlier in the initial encounter between two individuals, nothing much has transpired so you have a Non-Event. The relationship over time, an hour, a month, a year, or a decade, will either get stronger or weaker based on what we do. Obviously, as Motivational Accelerators (MAs), we have a desire for speed in building the relationship. We want to engage only in activities that impact our customer. We call those actions: Accelerators.

Accelerator:

Anything that enhances your image in the eyes of the customer.

THOUGHTFULNESS, KINDNESS, CREATIVITY, INTEGRITY, APPEARANCE, GENEROSITY, SENSE OF URGENCY, COMMUNICATION SKILLS, EDUCATION, DISCIPLINE, ASSOCIATIONS, CREDIBILITY, ENERGY, PUNCTUALITY, PARTICIPATION, RESPONSIVENESS.

There are plenty more, but for now these will suffice. These behavioral traits, when introduced, usually engender a reciprocal positive reaction. The customer may not put you in his will, but Acceleration is taking place. You are scoring points.

ACCELERATING ACTIONS

Acceleration can be achieved a thousand different ways. Any action that sends the message to your customer that you are concerned with their well-being will score points. How many points you score is up to you.

The following list of Accelerating Actions can be modified or improved upon. You are only limited by your imagination and willingness to act.

> ⇨ Surprise pizza parties.

> ⇨ Periodic delivery of something to eat... the more creative the better. You score with thoughtfulness and creativity.

> ⇨ Make a birthday list of customers and their spouses...make a phone call, send cards, and/or flowers; candy for occasions - birthday, births, anniversary, sickness; bad day cards.

> ⇨ Free lesson of any kind...golf, tennis, skiing, etc.

> ⇨ Send an autographed poster/picture of a favorite personality.

> ⇨ Give a gift for their children. The size of the gift doesn't matter.

⇨ Do something thoughtful for someone they hold dear.

⇨ Use your network of friends to somehow get involved with your best customers.

⇨ Invite a customer over for a cookout.

⇨ Take a customer with spouse for dinner.

⇨ Get involved in sporting events such as softball or bowling leagues.

⇨ Send a music cassette of a buyer's favorite artist.

⇨ Send a post card to customers while on vacation.

⇨ Call a customer at home on the week-end just to chat.

⇨ Give "Be My Guest" dinner certificate.

⇨ Give video rental gift certificates.

⇨ Give movie tickets.

⇨ Award a trip to the Mall with a gift certificate.

⇨ Take a customer to their favorite sporting, arts, or entertainment event.

⇨ Bring in ice cream, Popsicles, or sodas on a hot day.

⇨ Give a plant.

⇨ Run sales contests.

⇨ Give periodic gift baskets of chocolates, fruits, teas, coffees, gum, or candy.

⇨ Buy lottery tickets. To keep interest at a sales meeting, open with "All of you have an opportunity to become a millionaire during this sales meeting."

⇨ Have a picnic lunch at customer's office.

⇨ Take a customer for a hot air balloon ride.

⇨ Buy theme park tickets.

⇨ Bring desserts for lunch time.

⇨ Give a subscription to weekly sports newspaper or other periodicals of interest.

⇨ Give home phone number to key customers for evening calls.

⇨ Use theatrical themes for driving home the important aspects of a presentation (i.e., Rambo outfit).

⇨ Involve customer support personnel, such as office managers and administrative assistants, in promotions and entertainment.

⇨ Give creative sales presentations. If you aren't creative, find someone who is to help you.

⇨ Bring a barbecue grill and have a cookout with your customer.

⇨ Send a post card if something reminds you of your customer.

⇨ Use personal thank-you notes.

⇨ Write letters commending your customers' employees.

⇨ Use handwritten notes with articles, clippings, items of interest, etc.

⇨ Order your customer personalized stationery.

⇨ Ask your customers that are publishing newsletters to allow you to contribute information.

⇨ Do a follow-up interview after shipping their first order, or any important piece of business. How did we perform after we took the order? Thank them for the business.

⇨ Arrange trips to your facilities/plant to educate your customer and show your hospitality.

⇨ Get to know customers' employees. Work to remember names.

⇨ When you are out of town, try to call from the airport to ask how everything is going, and that you called to say Hi!

⇨ Apologize to customers in writing for blatant mistakes, and follow up with a phone call.

⇨ Handle all complaints immediately. Correct the situation as quickly as possible.

⇨ Provide information on subjects pertinent to their business.

⇨ FOLLOW UP, FOLLOW UP, AND FOLLOW UP SOME MORE.

We defined Accelerator earlier. A Positive Impactor is strictly a more robust Accelerator. It creates an intense reaction. An Accelerator gains ground incrementally while a Positive Impactor is akin to a knockout punch or a home run.

Positive Impactor:

Anything that generates a dramatic change in perception.

SUPERIOR INTELLIGENCE, PHYSICAL PRESENCE, WEALTH, COURAGE, SPEED OF ACTION

Save a customer's life. What do you think their response will be the next time you ask them for an order?

A SNAKE'S HEAD FOR PEACE OF MIND

In June of 1971, I was commissioned a second lieutenant in the U.S. Army. My career path dictated I attend a number of combat arms schools to insure I was properly trained on my way to becoming an "American fighting man."

Most of the instruction was pretty uneventful until my final qualifying jump in Airborne School. I stood in the ready line, inside a C-130 cargo plane, waiting for the green light to go on indicating it was time to exit the aircraft. The plan dictated seventeen paratroopers must get out the door safely in nineteen seconds. Sixteen made it. A second lieutenant, we'll call Dave, didn't. I guess he missed the class on how to hold your static line (the cord that pulls your parachute open), because he let it run under his arm instead of over his shoulder... a critical mistake. Dave's static line, upon leaving the airplane, wrapped around his arm and held him to the plane hanging six feet below the jump door. The situation was potentially life threatening but had a happy ending. As Dave flapped in the wind, the pilot brought the plane around whereby the jump master cut the line so Dave could pull the rip cord on his reserve parachute. Dave hit the ground a little embarrassed but pretty much intact.

Three weeks later, I entered Ranger School. So did Dave. Described as the most brutal military training in the world, it appears the program exists for only one reason, physical and mental abuse.

Ranger instructors are legendary in their ability to pour sulfuric acid on open wounds. I remember our first formation. We were 220-strong, and in the eyes of the cadre, fresh meat. None fresher than Dave. You see, due to Dave's exhilarating airborne experience, he came into Ranger school a known commodity. I'm not sure how long our initial orientation took, but it seemed like 90% of it involved verbally assaulting Dave.

As a matter of fact, every day we had "attack Dave time." In that the program is virtually 24 hours a day, 63-straight-day affair, there was no escape. After three weeks, the class had grown weary of hearing about Dave. I know he felt even worse and that's when I found out Dave was a salesman. He understood Impacting and Timing.

The sale? Convince the instructors to leave him alone. I remember it as vividly as if it happened last week. We had just finished the Camp Darby skill training phase of the program and were preparing to move on to the mountain phase. We were pulled together for a survival class. One part of the instruction involved learning how to live off the land. We were shown what plants and animals were a good food source and how to prepare them. Killing a variety of creatures in front of the candidates punctuated the point that death and blood were an ever present reality of Ranger life.

The coup de grace of the experience mandated the termination of a giant black snake. As the instructor pulled the reptile from the canvas bag, its serpentine tongue lashed out while it coiled around the instructor's arm. He unsheathed his Ranger utility knife as Blackie awaited its trip to snake heaven. "Wait!," came a scream from the back of the class. "I want to kill that mother...!" We all turned to find Dave standing with a crazed look in his eyes. "It's yours," said the instructor. Rangers like aggressive behavior. Dave walked up, through a chorus of oohs and aahs, and grabbed the snake and knife. He stood there for a couple of seconds, threw the knife down, and aggressively inserted the snake's head into his mouth. He had a plan, but unlike successful salesmen, he hadn't done his homework.

Snakeskin is extremely tough. His front teeth were biting ferociously, but making no progress. The oohs and aahs quickly turned to ughs as the snake wrapped itself around Dave's neck.

Failure hadn't been part of the plan. A Postitive Impactor was quickly turning into Deceleration and you could see the look of fear in his eyes. God only knows what was going through his mind. Whatever his doubts, he now had such an adrenaline rush, nothing would stop him. He moved the head to the side of his mouth and chewed it to pieces. As he pulled the headless snake from his mouth, Dave received a standing ovation. We never heard about his parachute jump again. Dave closed the sale.

Note: For years, as a way of exhibiting machismo, Rangers have bitten the heads off chickens.

Chickens' heads come off very easily.

The inverse of Acceleration is Deceleration. Instead of scoring points through actions viewed favorably by the customer, deceleration occurs when negative behavior presents itself. The customer has no desire to grow the relationship. They want out of it.

Decelerator:

An action that diminishes your image in the eyes of the customer.

RUDENESS, LETHARGY, THOUGHTLESSNESS, IGNORANCE, ARROGANCE, POMPOSITY, ALOOF-NESS, MYOPIA, APPEARANCE, LACK OF FOLLOW-UP, SARCASM, TARDINESS.

The exhibition of any one of these traits will cost you, and if you indulge regularly in Decelerating behavior, your chances of establishing a meaningful partnership are virtually non-existent.

DECELERATING ACTIONS

Deceleration occurs anytime your performance impacts the customer negatively. Listed below are twenty actions that will have a deleterious effect on your relationship with your customer.

DECELERATORS

⇨ Not returning your customer's phone calls promptly.

People make phone calls for a reason! In many instances they are looking for a response to something that concerns them. When you don't return phone calls promptly, you are making a statement that their concerns are not a high priority with you. So many salesmen are so bad at returning phone calls quickly; if you do you will stand out. If you don't, the customer will find a salesman who will and give them your opportunities.

⇨ Making disparaging comments to your customer about your competition.

Your customer is buying from your competition for a reason! If they were bad, they probably wouldn't be a supplier. When you put down a competitor, you are putting down your customer. They make a conscious decision to give business to someone else. Earn the business on your strength, not someone else's weakness. Weak salesmen focus on what others can't do rather than what they can do.

⇨ Keeping your customer waiting.

Time is life's most precious commodity. No one has a right to take it from someone else. Be a fanatic about being on time and you will gain a reputation. Take time away from your customer, and they will most certainly take their time away from you. Your time is theirs, but if you think the inverse is true, think again.

⇨ Dropping by without an appointment.

If something is important enough to see your customer about, it only makes sense you alert them to a visit. They can then schedule you when it's best for them. When you just drop by, you stand a good chance of disrupting their day. If they then have to accommodate you because you are there, you'll lose points.

⇨ Asking your customer to pick up their portion of a check for food, drink, or entertainment.

Your customer's orders are your success. Without them you are unemployed. If they are worth associating with outside the office, they are meaningful enough to have you pick up the tab. Your generosity will be rewarded. Their orders serve many purposes. When you ask your customer to pay their way, you are telling them the relationship is a one-sided affair, and it centers around you.

⇨ Not responding immediately to a customer's request.

When you respond slowly you send many messages.

❶ You don't value their input.

❷ You're lazy.

❸ You're preoccupied.

❹ You're incompetent.

❺ You're not a valuable resource.

Do yourself a favor. Get on top of things quickly, and stay on them until the customer is satisfied with your response. They may not be happy with your answer, but if your response is swift, they will continue to call you.

⇨ Giving your customer inaccurate information.

Successful operations require good intelligence. If you provide bad information, you damage your customers ability to perform and your credibility. Very quickly, you will become worthless.

⇨ Being inconsistent in your selling methods.

There is something about the human being that yearns for consistency. Inconsistency catapults situations into turmoil. In order to develop a plan, people need to know what they can count on. They will almost always gravitate to salesmen and situations that are predictable.

⇨ Complaining to the customer when things don't go your way.

Generally, customers make decisions that are in their best interest. Hopefully, many of those decisions will favor you, but if they don't, complaining about them creates a perception you are more concerned with your well being than theirs.

⇨ Arguing with your customer.

When you argue with a customer, you are telling them you know more about the issue than they do. You may, but I would suggest you give what information you have on the subject without judgmental overtones. Upsetting the person who pays your mortgage will cost you points. It's their business, and they have a right to run it how they choose.

⇨ Asking for an order before you've performed.

In fairy tales you get something for nothing. In selling, performing for the customer is a prerequisite for future success. Asking for business before you've earned it says you are naive, greedy, and ignorant of the dynamics of selling. Insure you have held up your end of the contract. Then, when your customer gives you business, which they will probably take from someone else, they will feel good about it.

⇨ Not thanking your customer, on a regular basis, for business they are giving you.

No one wants to be taken for granted.

⇨ Showing a lack of self-discipline in your customer's presence.

Self-discipline is a highly admired trait. Lack of it creates a perception that situations can get the better of you. Customers like to do business with salesmen who are capable of controlling their environment. Excess, in any form, Decelerates relationships.

⇨ Showing displeasure when you do something for your customer that is not in your best interest.

Give and take is the nature of selling. Not every situation will favor you. If the relationship is healthy, the pendulum will always swing back. The image you should convey is: whatever is good for your customer, ultimately, is good for you.

⇨ Not communicating regularly with your customer about everything that impacts the relationship.

Salesmen are the communication link between their company and the customer. Good decisions cannot be made without timely, accurate information. Without a salesman's input, a customer's operation will experience paralysis. If you are not inputting intelligence, your customer will find an alternate source.

⇨ Telling your customer how to run their business.

In relating to your customer, never tell them anything. Respond to their requests for assistance, or suggest alternatives to their present mode of operation, but let them make the decision on how to run their business. I've found more often than not, ownership engenders a sensitivity about their actions that is not conducive to instructional input.

⇨ Giving in to your customer too quickly on issues that are important to you and your company.

Being a valuable resource to your customer means having knowledge in areas that transcend your customers frame of reference. Backing down quickly on issues creates a perception that your knowledge has little worth, or your reluctance to take a stand characterizes you as spineless. In either case, you lose.

⇨ Not understanding your customer's business.

In order to provide the kind of support your customer needs to be successful, you must have an in depth knowledge of their business. Without it, your attempts to help will be off target and of little value.

⇨ Showing inconsiderateness to any customer employee.

You never know what role a person plays in an organization. Treat everyone with respect and you won't have to worry that your efforts will be undermined by someone you mistreated when they surface as a key player. More importantly, treat everyone with consideration, because it's the right thing to do.

⇨ Taking your customer for granted.

There will always be plenty of competitors who will be happy to make your customer feel special. If you take them for granted, it's only a matter of time before you are on the outside looking in.

Timing is everything! Well, that may be a slight exaggeration, but certainly it has a lot to do with a salesman's success. The world we live in is becoming a pretty complex place and most people have a lot on their mind. Being able to recognize when someone is mentally with you is key to making an effective sales presentation. Trying to sell someone when the timing is wrong leads to immediate Deceleration.

ONE MARTINI TOO MANY

Not too long ago, while in Boston for an annual convention, I attended an industry cocktail party. I happened to be standing with two gentlemen, one of whom carried the title of president of a company that purchased in excess of a billion dollars worth of product a year. He had the capability of making any salesman an instant success.

Right in the middle of telling a joke, a tap on the back interrupted him. He turned to find an individual who introduced himself as the new sales representative that would be calling on his company. The salesman then started to promote some products his company had recently introduced. After about a minute, the president stated that sales presentations shouldn't be conducted at cocktail parties and suggested the salesman find a better forum to make his pitch. The president turned to me, rolled his eyes, and said, "Who is that idiot?" I suspect his lack of timing cost him dearly.

Sales success is not accomplished by brute force. Finesse always works better. Timing your presentation will make a world of difference in how it is received.

Some individuals are so ignorant of the human dynamics that govern interpersonal associations, they will attempt to close a sale even when they have indulged in Negative Impacting. They fail to recognize there are certain actions that are so disdained, that no one wants an association with that perpetrator. Call it a customer's "Hot Button." When it's triggered, something immediate and highly negative happens. No Sale!!

Negative Impactors:

COWARDLINESS, STUPIDITY, DISHONESTY, GREED.

PREPARE FOR SURPRISES

If you're evaluating my list of Accelerators, Decelerators, and Impactors, you might disagree with my categorization. For you, wealth is not a Positive Impactor, it's a Decelerator. Every wealthy person you've known was a jerk. Dishonesty is not a Negative Impactor. The environment in which you operate is full of dishonest people, so it's nothing worse than a Decelerator.

I've been surprised a number of times in my selling career by overestimating or underestimating the power of my ammunition. Usually it occurred because I hadn't done my homework or didn't have enough information available to execute properly. An orientation came quickly and I didn't leave with a pat on the back. Every now and then, I fell into serendipity.

AN ALTERNATIVE TO MANSLAUGHTER

A number of years ago, twelve to be exact, I had taken over as the Midwest regional sales manager at International Paper Company. Within days of assuming my responsibilities, I asked one of my sales representatives to accompany her on a sales call to an account she had just lost. (The names have been changed to protect the guilty.)

She gave me a briefing on the situation, told me they were our worst customer, and our potential for turning them around was zero. We landed in

Detroit, rented a car, and headed for the account. As we got closer, I could see that my sales rep was becoming visibly agitated by the thought of confronting two honor graduates of the Attila the Hun School of Purchasing.

It disturbed me to watch her emotional transformation. I recognized the fear in her face and couldn't believe it. How bad could this customer be? The sign on their roof gave me some indication. It must have been used in a past Super Bowl. The art deco monstrosity read, "World Headquarters." In that I knew they were a single location company, it appeared ego had gotten the best of them. Little did I know how much.

We sat in the lobby for an hour. They were sending me a message! Finally, the vice president of Operations, Mike Bhutto, summoned us. We walked into his smoke-filled, dimly lit gymnasium of an office, and there he sat behind a desk that approximated the size of our rental car. Everything about him repulsed me. I wanted to carry on the conversation from outside his office door, but two wooden chairs were placed strategically in front of him.

We sat down, he gazed at us, a kind of crazed look on his face, and then exploded. I had never experienced a more vitriolic tirade. This is a joke, I thought. It's all part of a regional initiation for the new manager. My sales rep had set me up. It didn't take long to realize she hadn't, and I recognized Bhutto had some serious emotional problems. His one-sided diatribe took everyone hostage; my sales representative, my company, and I were all guilty of the problems they were experiencing. They would never do business with us again and lawsuits were imminent.

As he continued, I had plenty of time to think about my next course of action. He hadn't come up for air. His all-encompassing verbal abuse went beyond reason, so I soon found myself getting very emotional. My blood pressure skyrocketed, and I started to reflect back on my years as an Army Ranger. I knew at least ten ways to kill someone. Which one would I use on Bhutto? The business no longer mattered. Hand grenades, M-16s, Claymore mines and C-4 explosives flashed in front of my eyes. I didn't care if I went to jail. Then, miraculously, I came to my senses. I wasn't a sales representative calling on the account. My business card said sales manager. I had to set an example. I would keep my cool. To this day, I don't know where my response to Bhutto's attack came from. I hadn't read Tony Parinello's *Selling to Vito*, and in many ways, still flew by the seat of my pants.

Something told me to compliment him. I had no reason for it but I did. When he finally stopped to catch his breath, I said, "Mike, let me commend you for saying what's on your mind. It's individuals with backbone that force suppliers to be better. Most people in dealing with a five-billion-dollar company would be afraid to speak their mind." After I had uttered those words, I could not believe they came from me. The Patron Saint of Selling wanted my career to continue.

I waited for his response. It seemed like an eternity. He must have been in shock. You could see him psychologically processing my comment. His face started to take on a softer look. His response, his incredible response was, "Steve, it's not that bad." Holy shit! It worked. I couldn't believe my ears. Something profoundly significant had just occurred and I didn't know why.

Subsequent training and experience has taught me why. The placement of a well-timed, well-articulated compliment is a powerful relationship building tool. About that time, Joe Flynn, the owner, entered the office. He physically wasn't as intimidating as Bhutto, but he had a look in his eye that was no less menacing. They had honed their Bad Cop, Bad Cop routine to a razor's edge. It was attack time for Flynn.

I wasn't going to wait. I learned in the Rangers to take the offensive. Should I pull out my bayonet? No, I decided instead to pull out another compliment. Bhutto introduced us, and as he and Flynn exchanged comments, Bhutto gave him a look that I interpreted as saying, "This guy is okay."

I seized the opportunity. Here it comes. "Joe, I want to commend you on your choice of vice president of Operations. Mike has forced International Paper to do things that run counter to standard operating procedures. He's tough, but he's fair." What nonsense. I was gagging as I said it but I'd received such a favorable response from my first compliment, I wanted to roll the dice again.

It worked! Flynn's ego had been stroked. His decision put Bhutto in that position. Complimenting Bhutto in front of the guy who paid his salary did wonders for our relationship. He now saw me as an ally. It didn't take long after that to get a consensus that maybe our two companies could work together. We followed up on a number of issues they presented and things were back on track shortly thereafter. To this day, thousands of sales calls later, my day in Detroit stands as one of my proudest sales moments. It all started with a compliment.

Spend enough time on your investigative pre-plan, and your use of Accelerating Actions will hit pay dirt. Remember that discussion on chemistry and psychology? There is variability in how people view things, and because of that, we will never be able to pinpoint precisely where we are on the Spectrum of Influence. It doesn't matter! What we are concerned with as salesmen is the trend. Is it up or down? Are we bonding with our customer or are our actions tearing the relationship apart? There is no optimum strategic selling plan — an optimal course of action works just fine.

SLIDE RULES AREN'T NECESSARY

We stated earlier it is difficult to measure behavior

in numerical terms, but not impossible. If we are going to decipher where we are in the relationship, we must, as best we can, quantify the situation. It's important to turn human activity into a form that is measurable. If we don't, it's difficult to see where we stand. In order to do that, a simple model has been created that allows you to track and grade your actions. It is nothing more than a scorecard, and your ability to gain or lose points comes directly from your use of Accelerators, Positive Impactors, Decelerators, and Negative Impactors.

If we are going to establish our position in the relationship, we need to measure our actions. I can think of no better way of measuring our performance than using the Base Ten numbering system. But instead of using all ten numbers, we will use only two – the numbers 5 and 10.

Don't be turned off by this simple approach. Not everything needs to be complicated. Others use it also. Computers operate on a similar principle. The speed at which they process information is a direct result of their use of the Binary system of numeration. They also use only two numbers, 0 and 1.

We could try to be more accurate by incorporating smaller increments of measurement, but it would only complicate the issue without providing any better data. You see, as I have stated, we aren't ever exactly sure the absolute impact our actions have, but it's my experience that individuals can tell, with some certainty, whether their behavior is being viewed positively or negatively.

The signals are everywhere. Does the customer appear pleased to see you? Do they engage in extended conversations or are their answers curt and icy? Do they return your phone calls? Have they done anything nice for you lately? Are you included or excluded in their program? Are they confrontational or agreeable?

Each action is a direct result of how they view your relationship. If you've been Accelerating, scoring points, customer interaction is a pleasurable experience. On the other hand, if Deceleration has been the principle component of your selling style, you're in trouble. How much trouble? You can figure it out using a Sales Acceleration Log (SAL).

SAL is nothing more than a tool that helps you keep a record of your behavior. As I've stated, we want to quantify what we do so we can measure it. When using SAL, there are four levels of scoring that will register — two positives and two negatives. Accelerators carry a weight of +5, Positive Impactors +10, Decelerators -5, and Negative Impactors -10. You need to establish a time frame for your actions. Did they occur over a week, a month, or a year?

Obviously, the longer the time between actions, the more diluted they become. Accelerators, over time, turn into Non-Events. Now that we've established these ground rules, let's take a look at how your influence might grow at an account.

To keep things simple, we will always start the exercise with no score, 0. When you've concluded the scoring, you can then add to or subtract from a previous total. Recognize the score we achieve from SAL has no other purpose than to determine a numerical value so we can plot it on the Spectrum of Influence. The running total determines whether you are Accelerating or Decelerating. Have we done enough to transcend the Non-Event and move forward, or are our actions having a negative impact?

When it comes to measuring sales performance, we can draw upon numerous analogies from other

SALES ACCELERATION LOG (SAL)				
DECELERATORS	**—**	**BAL**	**+**	**ACCELERATORS**
Did not follow up on a request	– 5	0	+ 5	Brought your customer a gift
Showed up late for a presentation	– 5	**+ 5**	+ 10	Helped his daughter get an interview
Argued over a pricing issue	– 5	**+ 5**	+ 5	Bought lunch after a big order
Didn't return a phone call	– 5	**+ 5**	+ 5	Helped them count inventory
		+ 10	+ 5	Sent them an article on something
		+ 15	+ 5	Helped an employee with their job
		+ 20	+ 5	Wrote a letter commending them
Totals	– 20	**+ 20**	+ 40	

professions. If you ever thought of being a criminal lawyer, you probably are aware of the Scales of Justice. With a slight modification, you have a Sales model.

Acceleration and Deceleration occurs in a variety of ways. What you think are insignificant actions, may not be. There are lots of ways to gain or lose points.

DECELERATION

Action	Score
1. We don't call the customer for an appointment, we just drop by.	- 5
2. Our appearance is a little rough.	- 5
3. We have no sales promotion tools, no information documents.	- 5
4. We have other things to do so we're impatient.	- 5
5. Our grammar isn't proper.	- 5
6. We are asked a question and have no answer.	- 5
7. We tell the customer we will get back with an answer that afternoon and it takes two days.	- 5
8. We know the answer will not please the customer so we lie to them. *	- 10
	____
	- 45

*An old adage expresses it very well: Lose your wealth, you've lost nothing. Lose your health, you've lost something. Lose your credibility, you've lost everything!!

Could we have done it differently? Let's see.

ACCELERATION

Action	Score
1. We show courtesy by calling for an appointment.	+ 5
2. We always dress for success.	+ 5
3. We never go anywhere without support material.	+ 5
4. We always show patience because customers are the key to success.	+ 5
5. We've developed excellent written and verbal skills.	+ 5
6. We don't have the answer but we make a call on the spot to get it.	+ 5
7. We have someone else call the customer to ensure they understood what was told them.	+ 5
8. We never lie to our customer. The truth, no matter how bad, is always better.	+ 5
	+ 45

Can you see how being able to measure behavior helps take the subjectivity out of your opinion on where you stand. In the first example, you are in a Decelerating mode. In the second, you are in Acceleration. You still may be a long way from an order, but the trend is up. Your score determines you are doing the right things.

We could come up with another hundred scenarios and the book would weigh a lot more, but the fundamentals wouldn't change. In all selling activities, there are right and wrong ways to do things.

Certainly the degree to which they are right or wrong is in large part due to how your customer views them. What are their values, past experiences, and objectives? All will play a part in how they react. You don't want to jump too quickly in sizing up your target. If the round peg is not fitting into the round hole...well, I think you get my drift.

DON'T WASTE AMMUNITION

Human beings are complex animals! More often than not, my first impression of someone is usually wrong, and if not wrong, incomplete. But with time and interaction, the substantive aspects of their personality come to the forefront.

Motivational Acceleration reduces wasted effort. Although it involves speed, it places a high priority on patience and planning. Acceleration, in many ways, is analogous to taking a trip. If you get in your car and just start driving, there is a chance you will take some wrong turns and possibly get lost. Wasted time. Wasted energy. If you buy a map and read it, whatever the initial cost in time and money will certainly be repaid in the course of your travel.

MAs know lots of ways to get things done. Great Accelerators are like magicians. As with any magic show, they need to know their audience's level of expectation. If they came to see a tiger disappear, they won't be satisfied with seeing a pigeon pulled from a hat. Understanding your audience is a necessity.

Over the years, I have probably given four hundred speeches. When I first started, I would prepare a speech based primarily on what I wanted to say. With experience and some negative feedback, I now speak on what I believe the audience wants to hear. The reaction is always better. The same holds true when trying to sell someone. The customer has certain feelings about the natural order of things. You are part of that order and need to adjust your behavior accordingly. If you are going to Accelerate, being in sync with their view is important.

I've found that most people are not an open book and a little analysis is required to discover what makes them tick. Therefore, Motivational Acceleration consists of five operational components:

⇨ Research

⇨ Observation

⇨ Experimentation
⇨ Identification
⇨ Implementation

All activities focus on the customer. We Research to gather information about them. Observation is needed to see if our intelligence is confirmed by their actions. Experimentation tests our hypotheses. Identification labels our prey and mandates a certain type of ammunition. (We never use anything more deadly than an A-Bomb.) Implementation involves all those customer directed actions that motivate them to play with us.

The process is iterative by nature. To move ahead we must test, evaluate, readjust, and implement. With experience, the time between testing and implementing is shortened. We acquire a feel for what will work and what won't.

We recognize there are cause and effect relationships between actions. Patterns of activity become clear and responses predictable. We score like a pinball wizard. Influencing others becomes child's play. Well, not quite. You see, none of this happens by just talking or thinking about it. It requires, and I'll say it again, effort on your part.

I know, if you could be assured, excuse me, no, guaranteed, that a Motivationally Accelerated Selling Program would give you much of what you want in life, you'd start it today. Effort would be no obstacle. Does your reluctance to get going involve trust. It wouldn't surprise me. How many miracle cures have there been? Are you impatient for results? I wanted everything yesterday too.

There was nobody more impatient than I twenty years ago. I was in a hurry to succeed, and in the absence of guarantees and my own ignorance, when I didn't see signs of immediate success I got bored or frustrated and moved on. I knew nothing about Motivational Acceleration. I didn't realize I needed to be out of the Non-Event before anything of any consequence was going to happen with my customer.

I knew I was well received, but I wasn't aware I was 30 points shy of Acceleration. Six accelerators would have done it. One day's effort. The brass ring was within my grasp. How did I know the Non-Event is only the birthplace of hopes and wishes? Closing sales happens elsewhere.

What Do Popcorn and Successful Selling Have in Common?

Records reflect popcorn was introduced by an Indian named Quadequina at the First Thanksgiving in 1621. I knew it wasn't in the Middle Ages. There were just too many things going on. You never knew when you were going to have to go off to war. It could be any minute.

You see, when you put corn kernels in a pan and put a fire under them, initially, nothing happens. They just sit there. Jiggle them around and still, by all external appearances, they look moribund, dead to the world. We know they aren't. Inside a reaction is taking place. The heat being applied is having an effect. We keep at it because we know, either through experience or instruction, that at some point the temperature of the corn will reach a level that requires it to pop.

As you know, all the corn does not pop at once because there is variability among kernels. But, once the popping starts, in a very short time frame, you have it... a bowl of popcorn.

In selling, the course of events is almost identical to popping corn. Customers are sitting there waiting to be energized. Great customers are not born, they are created. It is the salesman's job to apply enough heat to get the process started.

Initially, as Accelerators and Positive Impactors are introduced, it may appear like nothing is happening. There is no evidence the customer is going to buy the proposal. In their present state, their value is marginal, but if you can get them to pop, the main feature will be a lot more enjoyable. The MA knows, just as the corn popper does, that success is a function of time.

Although the situation looks dormant, growth is occurring. It just takes faith. You may have thought those corn kernels didn't change until the actual pop, but in fact they had. They began to swell right from the start.

Acceleration with another person occurs the same way. Initially the changes are very subtle.

They drop you a note. You're invited into their office. They are in no hurry to finish the conversation. They thank you for your time. You don't have the order but it's on its way. Just keep applying heat. The corn will pop.

Unfortunately for many salesmen, their selling approach is analogous to fishing with a drift net. They just hang around hoping they will catch something. Because they have no recipe for success, they are never really sure their actions are hitting the mark. They hope that what they are doing is working, but in the absence of concrete feedback (orders), an operational insecurity begins to grow. Now they are looking for any excuse to bail out. They want to find an easier target.

Someone told them that the lock that secures the door to the customer's heart could be opened with a church key. They were misinformed! There is no door. The entryway is unobstructed. In my twenty years of professional selling, I can't recall a situation where I did not have access to the person I wanted to sell. The initial encounter may have been brief, and I may have blown the opportunity to move ahead, but never has anyone raised their hand and said, "Stop. I don't want to hear what you have to say."

The reason is obvious. Intelligent people recognize that in virtually all things, there are better alternatives, and one way of finding out about them is through human interaction. Hearing someone else's story can be highly informative and rewarding. People want to be sold, but they will decide who sells them!

Your challenge in Selling at Mach 1 is not unlike walking through the English garden maze at the start of this chapter. There is an open entry and exit. Successful navigation involves nothing more than finding the correct path. With proper instruction, you will enter and exit quickly. You know that many of the paths that present themselves lead to nowhere. You know not to take them. Time and effort will be saved.

The inverse is you've been given no guidance and no map. Every choice is an experiment — a guess. Every path is taken to its unproductive end. Energy is wasted. A wrong turn and you are back where you started — frustrated and worn out. Quitting looks like an inviting option to starting over. There must be a better way.

Frank, why the donuts?

INFLUENCE A POSITIVE PERCEPTION

*To reject the idea that nothing holds
greater value than true friendship is
to have never had a true friend.*
— Sam Sebastiani

In 1978, after reading an article in *Forbes* magazine about getting ahead in business, I decided to enroll at the University of Southern California to earn a master's degree.

What I thought would be an educationally rewarding and productive experience turned out to be one of the most painful periods of my life. No, there weren't any night parachute jumps, no twenty-mile forced marches, and the full equipment five-mile Ranger runs were a thing of the past. The pain manifested itself as mental anguish. Not because getting a master's degree in systems management is particularly difficult; the suffering comes from knowing that what you are learning has very little utility in the real world. It's painful when you realize all those hours of discussion and study will probably never be applied, at least not in selling.

The empiricism required to build a bridge is not needed in building a relationship. The universal truths that enable scientists to put satellites in orbit do not apply in getting a customer to put their signature on an order form. It happens only when they feel good about their situation and you as the salesman.

Their perception about all things great and small triggers actions that either reward or punish your performance. The only reality that exists takes residence in the customer's mind and it determines where the relationship goes. Their reality must become your reality.

If you are going to develop an emotional bond with your customer, there is nothing more important than creating an image that impacts favorably on their consciousness. People act on what they see.

GENESIS 101

At the beginning of any relationship, your initial behavior creates an impression that the customer, at some future date, acts upon. Are your actions in harmony with how they see things, or are they a cacophonous collection of miscues? Do you project an image of a person with integrity, knowledge, sense of urgency, commitment, and compassion, or do your ill-advised periodic departures from common courtesy paint a picture of you as an unprofessional dolt?

If you are having difficulty in your selling endeavors, there is a good chance you lack a fundamental understanding of the importance of creating positive perceptions.

I can tell you from firsthand experience that many individuals who have ascended to the highest levels in our society are severely lacking in a number of humanistic attributes. They aren't particularly smart; they're selfish, abusive, predisposed to egoism, and in many cases, insecure. On a scale of one to ten, they are, at best, a three.

It's difficult these days to pick up a paper and not read about someone we've idolized being knocked off their pedestal. It shocks us to find out that the emotional makeup of the private person is far different from the public person. How did they get so far?

It's easily explainable. They learned how to influence perceptions. The majority of their overt behavior was characterized by good deeds. They forced themselves to do things that their audience liked, and in doing so, established an image that others wanted to support. Their shortcomings only took the stage behind closed doors.

Now, for every maladjusted miscreant that has

made it to the top through deception, there are a hundred that got there legitimately. But I suspect they were no less aggressive in portraying their positive attributes while keeping less desirable tendencies undercover.

It just makes sense. People do not want a relationship with someone whom they view negatively. The more your actions parallel someone else's view of how they think things should be, the quicker your emotional bond will become.

Some Facts About Impressions

❶ They are created almost instantaneously.

❷ First impressions die hard.

❸ Everything you do makes a greater or lessor impression than you think.

❹ Actions impress far more than rhetoric.

Very few buyers develop strong relationships with salesmen whose behavior runs counter to what they think is correct. The Motivationally Accelerated relationship is one in which the salesman identifies what is important to the buyer and displays behavior that ties to it.

Did you know buyers :

⇨ Want to feel they are special.

⇨ Expect quick responses to their requests.

⇨ Love creativity.

⇨ Admire courage.

⇨ Disdain deceit.

⇨ Need consistency.

⇨ Hate excuses.

⇨ Are generally fair.

⇨ Will always find a way to give business to someone they like.

⇨ Want to do business with people who are successful.

Did you know that Motivational Accelerators:

⇨ Place their customers on a pedestal.

⇨ Are imprisoned by their desire to do what the customer wants.

⇨ View no request as too small or too big to be acted upon.

⇨ Are always differentiating themselves from their competition.

⇨ Remind their customers regularly through acts of thoughtfulness and generosity how important the relationship is to them.

⇨ Are incapable of deceit.

⇨ Know their business.

⇨ Are considerate, consistent and credible.

⇨ Believe their response to any situation can never be too quick.

⇨ Are consumed by a desire for results.

I'm well aware that you bought this book because you want to sell better. You are also hoping that much of what you learn will identify activities that make a greater impact while requiring less effort.

Those are my feelings exactly. I have no desire to spend long periods of time accomplishing something. Quick and easy is always better. What matters is results!

There is a difference between efficient and effective. Most bureaucrats are very efficient but highly ineffective. That's the reason, when dealing with government, it takes so long to get things accomplished.

As a salesman looking to make an impact, there are certain attributes that are required to Accelerate situations. Hopefully, they are presently part of your makeup. If not, you should work on acquiring them. But no attribute, regardless of how wonderful, is of any use to you if the customer does not observe it. They will only respond to what they see. Given that, it's imperative you display as many of your positive characteristics as you can while refraining from showing your warts. Accelerate, don't Decelerate. MAs do things that help them project an image that the customer feels good about. I could give you a hundred examples but I think you're smart enough to grasp the concept with one.

A EUROPEAN SPORTS CAR FOR 69 CENTS

Do you want customers to think you care about them? It's a rhetorical question, of course you do. Is that the perception you create when you do something for them during a business day? Possibly, or maybe not. Customers aren't stupid! Whatever you do during work hours ties directly to your desire to get something from them. They know it and therefore your actions are more self-centered than customer directed. No points.

If you're an Accelerator, your concern is genuine and you want them to know it. It's important they think they're never far from your thoughts. Even during your vacation, a period when you should be relaxing and enjoying your time away, they are with you. So you let them know by sending a post card or maybe even a small gift to express your feelings. It costs virtually nothing in time and effort, but the impact is substantial. Your thoughtfulness is not viewed as a setup for another order, but rather it's interpreted as a thank-you for the business. Major score.

Over the years I've observed hundreds of salesmen in action. Many of them worked very hard at being successful. They failed! They never figured out how the game was played. It wasn't what they were that mattered; it got down to what the customer thought they were. They were never able to look at themselves from their customer's point of view. They knew nothing about Motivational Acceleration. They had no idea that stupid actions cost them points. For every Accelerator they employed, they negated it with a Decelerator. They stayed in the Non-Event.

For some unknown reason they thought their customers would accept substandard performance. Their Accelerators would be rewarded while their Decelerators would be quickly forgiven and forgotten. Using that kind of logic, they will spend their selling career adrift in the doldrums.

Perceptions are easily influenced. If you need a guidance mechanism to keep your efforts on track, I suggest you use the Golden Rule. It's not much more complicated than that.

TWO TACOS FOR BROTHER STEVE

John Matos, owner of a chain of Mexican restaurants in Connecticut called Panchos and Gringos, understands the concept perfectly. There are lots of Mexican restaurants around that serve good food and drink but there are none whose owner makes you feel so overwhelmingly welcome that you start to believe you are a relative. From the moment you walk through his doors and he greets you, his warmth and friendliness makes an impression. You're not sure whether he is your brother, father, or mother. It doesn't matter. You're family! Now when decision time rolls around and you are making your choice for a Friday night fiesta, are you going to go to a stranger's for margaritas or Uncle Johnny's?

I once attempted to go elsewhere four years ago, and I felt like Benedict Arnold. The guilt almost killed me. John Matos gives me two hours worth of attention in the course of a year of dining at Panchos and Gringos, and I give him $15,000. A terrific financial return by anyone's standard.

Does influencing positive perceptions pay? Someday I expect the NFL will ask John to play the Super Bowl in his backyard.

SPEED OF ACTION

I hope I live to be a healthy one hundred and fifty years, because only then will I have had as much fun and accomplishment as I want.

If the nature of living a life was a bit different I could probably do it all in 10 years. That will never happen though because of interactivity, "Dead Time." You know what I'm talking about; that time between finishing one thing you enjoy until the start of something else that is significant. Boy is there a lot of it.

I ski, but sometimes I wonder why. In the course of an 8-hour day of skiing at Squaw Valley, California, on a typical Saturday, my skis are only going down the mountain for fifty-two minutes. The rest of the time is waiting; for parking, lift tickets, chair lifts and lunch. I don't like it, and I don't know anyone who does. I've noticed a direct correlation between success and a desire in individuals to limit dead time.

If you haven't figured it out yet, successful people are in a hurry! They don't try to get from one point to another by bus. They are looking to catch a rocket ship. Their epitaph will not read "They died from administrative overload." The word "static" is not in their vocabulary. They will find the vehicle to get them where they want, ex post haste.

Whether you are perceived as a Yugo or a Ferrari is up to you. If they ask for assistance with something, don't wait. Do it the second the request is made. If you delay, no points are scored. If you excuse yourself and tell them you need to make a phone call to get it accomplished, voila, you've just exhibited, through action, what is important to them is important to you. All of a sudden a Positive Impactor shows up on your score card.

Do I need to explain what moving at 10 MPH will do for your career. I think not. I do not remember one individual who I've called on who was not impressed by a sense of urgency. Carry with you an attitude that nothing can be done too swiftly, and you've taken a quantum leap forward in securing your selling success.

APPEARANCE

The human brain is an incredible piece of physiological machinery. At its lowest level of cognitive performance, it accomplishes remarkable things. Unfortunately, very little of its output is ever seen.

The only way anyone will know the depth of your thoughts is when they appear through action. You will be measured by what you say, how you look, and what you do. The essence of a human being is cognition but acceptance is a product of physical acts. If that is the case, then cover all your operational bases; look, act, and speak like a professional. Translated, that means don't settle for less than you are capable of providing.

Did you know perceptions are easily influenced?

⇒ Wearing a fake Rolex watch creates a perception you are unsuccessful and deceitful.

⇒ Poorly shined shoes reflects on your attention to detail.

⇒ An unattractive business card means you don't understand the communication process.

⇒ Not returning phone calls shows lack of concern.

⇒ Not saying please and thank-you portrays egotism and bad manners.

⇒ Taking without giving paints a picture of parsimony.

⇒ Dominating behavior depicts insecurity.

If you've ever thought that the less desirable aspects of your behavior go unnoticed, I would suggest you reevaluate. The same behavioral shortcomings that you find distasteful, others will have trouble swallowing also.

If you are naive enough to believe Decelerators will be overlooked or forgotten, you will probably spend many a future vacation at the bowling alley.

LET SOMEONE ELSE FINANCE YOUR DREAMS

There is only one good thing about a long commute to work; you have plenty of time to think. In 1986, I'd thought through most of the world's problems, and had just finished reading an article about the money to be made in the apparel industry. I decided I wanted to become a Rag Man. I would create a name, develop high-quality innovative sports apparel, find someone to manufacture it, and sell a zillion.

I had the name, Osoli. The company would initially produce the finest sports cap made, so it was imperative I find a worldclass manufacturer. The plan seemed simple enough. Unfortunately, high quality manufacturers weren't walking the streets looking for business. They were already working for Ralph, Donna, and Calvin. Convincing them to make products for a company that had no track record, without a major monetary investment up front, was as easy as swimming through the La Brea tar pits. Many of my calls went unreturned, and when I did get through to someone, they weren't interested. They already had Hugo Boss.

Being a novice in the business, I didn't understand how things worked. Then it came to me. At the end of a phone line, I sounded like everyone else. I had no recognizable name, no credibility, and no success. How many similar calls did they receive in a week? To risk a large capital investment with anyone before I even had a viable program seemed stupid. Either they would do it or it wouldn't get done. I had to adopt an In-Your-Face, selling strategy. The plan? Show up at their office and let my appearance do a lot of my talking for me. I did know how to Sell at Mach 1, so getting through the receptionist would not be a problem.

The plan was pretty straight forward. I would communicate my objective, what Osoli was about, and what part they could play in this apparel success story waiting to happen. I needed Accelerators. I had a red and black Porsche Targa with a whale tail. Five points. My closets were full of suits, but nothing that shouted, "Villa in St. Moritz." I purchased a double-breasted suit that cost almost as much as the car. Five points. Accessories were also important. I didn't care for alligator shoes but they did make a statement. I found a pair at half price, $400. Five points. All I needed now was a Positive Impactor. Something that would scream, "Money! Success! Accomplishment!" I decided the Coup de

Grace to my look would be a $12,000 Rolex President with a plain black onyx face and jubilee band. Beautiful! Ten points. It was easy to justify because I had wanted the watch for years. Now it would pay for itself.

Long story short, all of the sudden everyone thought Osoli was a great idea and they wanted to participate. A number made financial investments in equipment to get me started. They developed my products at their cost. Within months, Osoli was up and running.

Something triggered a change in attitude, and to this day I believe much of it had to do with appearance. At the other end of a phone line, my appearance was anything their mind conjured up. No sale! When I sat in front of them, speculation was removed. The car, the suit, the shoes, and the watch were a reality. I must have been a success. They wanted to grab my coattails. I might be wrong, but I'm not going to call Shelly Luna of Atlas Headware to find out. I'd hate to think those alligator shoes I haven't worn since were a waste of money.

ASSOCIATIONS

I was asked recently to identify my greatest selling asset, and without a moment's hesitation I replied, "Growing up all over the world."

When you've lived in twenty-nine places in forty-four years, you have had countless associations with people, places and things. It's been a long time since I've been with someone that I didn't share some common ground. There is an old adage, "You are known by the company you keep." Expand that concept, and we could say that our associations give insight into who we are.

As MAs, we want our customers to feel good about us. If we delivered a monologue about the essence of our goodness, it would be long-winded, self-serving, and tiresome. You won't need to. Let your associations do the talking. It is a far quicker way to influence a perception.

Each association, in whatever form it takes, carries with it a history and reputation. In most associations, your connection came about by choice and therefore, whatever image it carries will, in some way, be projected to you. Right or wrong, it happens.

Your customers have associations also. When their interests coincide with yours, Acceleration takes place. Deceleration occurs when your associations come in conflict.

I GOT MY KICKS ON ROUTE 66

In retrospect, it served as a great learning experience, although at the time I viewed it as anything but educational.

On February 15, 1977, I had just been given my DD Form 214, indicating my resignation from the Army had been accepted and "Soldier" no longer described my occupation. Corporate America awaited me in San Francisco and I had five days to get there.

My BMW 3.0CS could cruise at 130 MPH, so maybe I would do the trip in a day and a half. Whatever the time frame, I knew I would exceed the speed limit, so I strategically hung my class A Army uniform in the back window. I'd discovered a few years earlier, state troopers had a sympathetic soft spot for army officers. I think it had something to do with protecting the country or a shared value system of guns, Mom, and apple pie. Whatever their thinking it engendered an attitude of "Give the speeder a break" and with a 2800 mile journey ahead of me, I thought I might need a few breaks.

In looking at the map, I decided to take historic Route 66 across the country. As I blew through city after city, I began to realize the TV series had overstated the adventure to be found along the roadway. I would be in Oklahoma City in an hour and hadn't had a thrill yet. After fourteen hours of driving, weariness had set in, and I decided to look for a motel. By the time I found one, my watch said 0100 hours and they were closed for the night. I had a sleeping bag in the trunk so I really didn't care. I would find a rest area near the highway and save twenty dollars. I got off at the next exit and proceeded optimistically down a country back road. I knew the perfect spot would be found right around the bend.

Thirty miles up the road, my optimism gone, I

decided the location no longer had to be perfect. It only had to accommodate the length and width of my car. Within seconds of having changed the criteria for my sleeping accommodations, a dirt road appeared to the left. It looked inviting. As I pulled in my lights illuminated a fence and an open gate. A sign on the fence post said, not surprisingly, "No Trespassing."

It runs counter to my value system to violate someone's right to privacy, so initially, I had no intention of entering the field beyond the fence, but lack of sleep does funny things to the mind. The clock on the dashboard now read 0200 hours and I started to rationalize that "No Trespassing" only applied to people who were planning on homesteading. I would only be there a couple of hours. Hell, I'd spent the past six years protecting their lifestyle. I had an entitlement.

I would pull in just far enough so I wasn't visible from the road. Within moments of entering the property, I detected something wasn't right. The night radiated a cold, damp blackness...and my tires were spinning in the mud. I immediately turned off the engine and got out of my car to see what had transpired. I pulled out a flashlight and as I turned it on, a sickening feeling overcame me. The two rear tires had just dug the Erie Canal in some farmer's cornfield. My German friend and I were stuck!

After going through the alphabet of epithets, I decided I would confront my predicament in the morning. I pulled out my sleeping bag and crawled in.

I guess I fell asleep immediately, because I don't remember anything until excruciating pain brought me to consciousness. My ribs felt like they had exploded. This is a dream, I thought. The next blow to my buttocks assured me it wasn't.

Four-letter words seemed to be coming from all directions. Dazed, I climbed out of my bag and stood up. The light shown in my eyes blinded me and an object was immediately pressed against my cheek. For all I knew it could have been a broom stick until a voice thundered, "Move and I'll blow your f...ing head off." Over the next few minutes, they called me every conceivable derogatory name. Both gentlemen were working themselves into a frenzy. I probably would have been more frightened had I not been in so much pain.

I told them I hadn't seen the "No Trespassing" sign. At that point the individual with the gun against my face stated, "We shoot trespassers around here." I'd hoped he said that for effect.

As I stood in my underpants, wondering where is this situation headed, the second gentlemen searched my car. Immediately, he saw my uniform hanging in the back window. "Are you in the Army?" he inquired. I quickly evaluated my choices for a response and lied, "Yes, I'm on my way to Fort Sill." Immediately something caught his interest. "Are you airborne?" he asked. He knew the answer the moment he saw the parachutist badge on my uniform. "Yes," I said. "I was airborne. I spent two years in the 82nd," he stated.

All of a sudden silence blanketed us. You could feel him processing my input. "I'll be back when it's light to pull you out," he said.

As quickly as it begun, the encounter ended. They were gone within moments. At daybreak, he showed up and pulled my car out. Virtually, no words were exchanged. No apology was given.

I suspect he didn't like me much more than the night before, but because we were members of the same club "Paratrooper," he felt an obligation to assist me. Periodically, I reflect back on the experience and wonder what would have happened had I put my uniform in the trunk.

Associations are a great catalyst to get Acceleration started. Everyone is looking for common ground. It helps with the communication process. It allows you to interface in an area where you both have knowledge. The concept is pretty simple to understand. A friend of a friend is a friend, but it can also lead to Deceleration; associating with enemies creates enemies.

INSIDER OR OUTSIDER

As you evaluate your own inventory of associations, recognize you don't have to be a fellow delegate to the United Nations to cement a relationship. In most instances a change in perception will start to occur the moment another individual realizes you have something in common.

I've shown up at business meetings in West Texas dressed like a Wall Street banker, and when I sat down at the table on a scorching July afternoon, the temperature at the table was frigid. I was an outsider and I'm sure they thought I looked like a charter member of the Quiche Club.

West Texas is rough and tough. Clint, red meat, and Harley Davidson are king. No sissies allowed! When I start to break the ice with casual conversation, do I talk about my interest in art, classical music or tennis? It depends on the audience, but in this situation, those subjects are associational playing cards that will not be dealt.

I'm interested in scoring points not losing them. Sunday morning rides on my Harley, pumping iron at the gym, or pulling the trigger on a Canadian goose, now that's what life is all about. It seldom fails. In a short period of time, I'll go from what initially felt like the Arctic tundra to a beach in Maui. The relationship heats up.

I've known salesmen who had no success at selling a buyer, no matter how hard they worked, until it became evident they shared a meaningful association. That association was the ignition spark that got the relationship moving.

In that you want to get going in the right direction, I recommend you do a little investigative research. Find out about your customer's interests, likes and dislikes. Never forget the tendency with many is to look for the worst in people instead of the best. Don't give your buyer an excuse not to do business with you.

In the late seventies when I called on accounts in Berkeley, California, did I ever bring up my military background? On one occasion I did and as the relationship did an immediate "about-face" and marched out of my life, I realized the *National Association of Printers Against the Vietnam War* would never link arms with *Rangers for a Scorched Earth.*

I now try to feel out my customer before I put my mouth into gear. I don't know if I'll ever make a call on Mothers Against Hell's Angels, but if I do and I'm asked what I do for fun, I'd be tempted to say, "I drive my station wagon."

A Picture Is Worth More Than 1000 Words

There are many challenges when you work in New York City, none bigger than finding a great new deli to eat lunch.

It normally happens two ways: a co-worker makes a suggestion, or you walk the streets until some gastronomic indicator tells you this is "the place."

Actually, there was a time when there was three ways. The third is you would call Telly Savalas and ask him. You see, Telly had eaten in every deli in New York. At least, I think he had. Why else would his picture be in all their windows. It had even appeared in a pet-food store. Did Telly actually eat there or was it his Rottweiler?

It does get confusing. What about that window that showcased Telly, Orson, and Dinah. Were they all there together? How did Dinah like her Reuben? It must have been great or she wouldn't have given them her picture. Or did she?

It wasn't until one October afternoon when I stepped in to grab a bite at Otto's Dim Sum that I started to suspect that framed photos on the wall didn't necessarily mean an endorsement. When I received my moo goo gai pan, and it tasted like dog food, I figured it out.

Frank Sinatra's words came crashing down on me. "If you can make it there, you can make it anywhere." How true. The competition is fierce. To survive in the Big Apple, you have to use every available resource. Why not Kojak?

Is it deceptive? I think not. It's called promotion. If you are going to Accelerate, you had better learn how to promote yourself. If you can't, you'll spend your life running with the pack.

It is widely known that individuals want to associate with successful people. Call it the Coattail Principle. If you influence a perception of success, others will want to hang on for the ride. They will try to use you, and in return you will find ways to use them. Nothing wrong with that. It's called Life.

Putting a celebrity photo in your window is the pictorial equivalent of being a name dropper. As with anything, you should manage the process. Moderation works better. Dropping one or two names in the course of an evening with your customer is smart selling. You'll score points. Overkilling the technique will get you labeled as a bore. You'll Decelerate quickly.

Most people have a tendency to make great assumptions with very little information. When you provide the perfect "jewel" at the right time, their brain will take off on an intellectual marathon, and when it's finished, you may have conquered the world or at least their part of it.

Do You Know Tommy Ferrentino?

In my business career, I have encountered few individuals as talented as Kim Rendelman. Her resume is a headhunter's dream, and in the ten years I've known Kim, I've watched her rise to the highest levels of corporate America. As vice president of Marketing at International Paper, she was always accepted and included in whatever arena she was operating in, with one exception. Kelsey's Gym.

You see at Kelsey's, the in-crowd is part of the CEPS gang. If you didn't have bulging biceps, triceps and quadriceps, you were in the out-crowd. I've been lifting weights since I was twelve so I could appreciate her predicament. Anyone who has ever taken weight training seriously understands that being an outcast makes the gym experience far less rewarding. When that lactic acid enters your muscles after thirty repetitions, and your arms are burning, you need a muscle head calling you a wimp to spur you on. Kim had none.

She had gotten the weight lifting bug a few years earlier and for some reason wanted her physical prowess to match her mental capability. Brains and Brawn – what a deadly combination. Sadly enough, she did not inherit the "muscle gene." After a couple months of working out on her own, she realized she would never achieve what she wanted in strength conditioning unless she could work out with the "Big Boys." The situation appeared hopeless because the only criterion they used was physical appearance. Muscle mass meant everything and Kim had little. What she did possess was an understanding of the power of association.

Kim understood the concept perfectly. She knew about my friendship with Tommy Ferrentino, one of the world's top body builders. She asked me if I could get Tommy to sign one of his body shots. He did. It read "Kim, you are my motivation. Tommy."Somehow that photo found its way to the gym and the CEPS gang. They had no idea Kim knew Tommy. If Kim knew Tommy she must be something special. How could she possibly be Tommy Ferrentino's motivation? Obviously, there was more to her than met the eye. Did she also know Cory, Lee, and Arnold? Would she bring them to the gym? It's not surprising Kim is now a member of the in-crowd. No, I don't know what will happen when Arnold never shows up.

THAT SUITCASE ISN'T MINE

Yes, it is! I've said when you enter into a relationship you start with a Non-Event. Well, not exactly. Your initial encounter with a buyer may be a Non-Event because you just met, but in the course of their association with your company and all its ancillary entities, there is a history. As the salesman on the account, you are responsible for the sum of everything the customer feels about the relationship. It comes with the job description. Good, bad, or indifferent, their feelings belong to you.

You thought you started on a level playing field. Life's a bitch! Previous sales representation, quality problems, and lack of responsiveness have you sliding through the visitors' end zone. The word is out. Your organization and anyone associated with it is a leper. You just got there and you're down 900 points. Implosion isn't far away.

If you want to make an impact, there's no time like the present. Excess baggage is a killer! On the upside, I've found customers to be quite forgiving (The sins of the father shall not be visited on the son), but only if an immediate program of change is implemented. Action, not rhetoric, is essential! First impressions are critical so everything needs to be quickened. Overkill in the first six months is necessary. It will cement in the customer's mind, you are different. An overabundance of attention, follow-up, and sense of urgency will help counter a legacy of abuse. Don't expect any orders, but if you play your cards right, you'll probably get back to the Non-Event. From there, one tank of jet fuel and you are on your way.

NOTES

Not related.

SHE LOOKED
LIKE ZORRO

*I've always found it is easier to ride a bucking
bronc in the direction it's going.*
— Cowboy Frank Ginolfi

Appearances are deceiving.

Just ask Victor Hugo. The Hunchback of Notre
Dame was a wonderful guy. He would have been
the life of any Parisian cocktail party, but he never
received an invitation. It's not surprising, because
until you know differently, you act on what you see.

My experience in dealing with others has edu-
cated me to the fact that people are dramatically
different than the image they project. With age and
experience, I've gotten much better at not jumping
to conclusions about someone until I've observed
their behavior over a period of time. I've been surprised so often, I've come to the realization that
there is a Cosmic Law that governs the creation of

first impressions. They are never correct.

I'll use myself as an example. I believe there is no one who puts a higher price on friendship than I. There are many who place an equal price on it. I hold friendship in such high regard I direct a tremendous amount of energy and time to my friends. Because of this, I can only accommodate so many. I want to make sure that before I bring them into my inner sanctum, they are worthy of the consideration they will receive.

When I first meet someone, I am cordial but reserved. I probably come across as distant, but I'm not. I just believe that friendships are developed through experience not rhetoric. When your actions indicate to me you understand the give and take of a friendship, I'll be happy to be your friend. I would hope your customers operate the same way. They save their business for the salesman that is willing to put effort where his mouth is. You are in competition with lots of others who want the same thing you do. It seems reasonable to me why a buyer would not immediately embrace you. You haven't been tested. I've found the quicker a relationship is established, the less value there is in it.

A problem many salesmen encounter is a tendency to judge someone quickly and then act on their initial feelings. I suggest you indulge in a little analysis before you do anything. Become a practicing psychologist. Ignore what comes out of someone's mouth; it's probably part of their act, their facade. Watch their actions; they are the key to what makes them tick.

Do not lump your buyers into one collective bag and sell them all the same way. If you do, you will connect with a few but miss with the rest. People are different and unique. Psychologists have identified them in a variety of ways, with numbers, letters and adjectives. A lot of it makes sense. Much of it doesn't.

In my simple way of relating to all those different personalities out there, I place people in one of two categories:

❶ Giver

❷ Taker

Neither is meant to carry any negative connotation. I know a lot of wonderful people who are predominantly takers. They give, but their psychological orientation finds more pleasure in receiving. They do require a different selling strategy. Tactics need to be developed.

A Giver will allow the sale to occur if the salesman is performing because they enjoy giving something back. A Taker will do the same thing for a salesman, but their motivation is different. They give in order to receive. If accommodating you gets more for them, you will be accommodated. The carrot and stick approach works very well with Takers.

Thoughtfulness and consideration are excellent attributes to employ with Givers. Givers want a relationship for the relationship's sake. To give, they need someone they like to give to.

Takers, on the other hand, are like the Cookie Monster. They have an insatiable appetite. They want to know if the cookie jar is full.

There is a dramatic difference in my selling style when calling on a Taker versus a Giver. My technique changes because in order to Accelerate, you need to adapt to the personality of the buyer.

Introducing a chameleonesque approach to your selling style is appropriate. That doesn't make you shallow. I'm not suggesting you compromise on principle, just tactics. When I spend time with Givers, the topic of discussion centers around the things that are important to me and hopefully them: trust, giving, honesty, generosity, and compassion. When I'm with a Taker, the conversation takes on materialistic overtones. I want them to know I have lots of "cookies" in the jar. They can use my Porsche, borrow my Harley Davidson, get clothed by Osoli, and visit Connecticut where accommodations, food, and entertainment await them.

I've found Takers want to use me, and that's great. I just make sure they understand there is a cost associated with everything. On the other hand, Givers want to be used, and your biggest challenge is to guard against taking too much.

I enjoy being Santa Claus, but when I feel it is a one-way street, I'll put in a few speed bumps. Motivationally Accelerated relationships gravitate toward...balance. Our credo: When you take...give. When you give...take.

It's such an uncomplicated world!

Notes

Thanks, Amanda. Let's double that order.

PERSONALIZING
RELATIONSHIPS

Be liked and you will never want.
— Arthur Miller

In the course of getting to this stage in my life, I've been involved in a number of high risk ventures. I've jumped out of airplanes in the middle of the night, repelled from helicopters, kayaked through class-eight rapids, cliff dove, and started my own apparel business.

Each situation in its own unique way terrified me, but nothing generated more fear than starting a business relationship with John Clifford.

James Bond? No, John Clifford. A lot of people confuse the two. The adjectives are similar: debonair, worldly, precise, professional, caring, knowledgeable, and lethal. That's right, lethal; James in the world of espionage, and John in the world of business. Both always get their man; forgive me, person.

Do you think I'm exaggerating the case. You decide. In 1985, John Clifford started his own company, Clifford Paper. Nine years later, it is a $300 million enterprise and growing rapidly.

Let's put that in perspective. Harvey McKay, the decade's foremost authority on selling, had a $30 million company when he wrote *How to Swim With Sharks and Not Get Eaten*, a national best seller. His company, McKay Envelope, is now around $35 million. If numbers mean anything, you might surmise that John was the captain of Harvey's swim team. John says no, and I guess it doesn't matter. What does matter are the methods Clifford uses to accomplish his goals.

His formula for success is simple. He establishes contact, arranges a meeting, begins to make you feel there is nobody in the world more important than yourself, and then asks for the order. You give it gladly because his transition from salesman to friend is so smooth, you would tell your mother "No" before Clifford.

The logic behind his actions is not revolutionary. He knows, as do all MAs, that making your customer your friend is smart business. They become more open, loyal, consistent, and credible than when they were strangers. It requires time and effort outside the normal nine to five business day.

Why is it critical to be involved with someone after business hours? Remember the discussion on perception? Customers are not stupid. They perceive, when you interact with them while they're working, that your actions are self-centered. Your performance has one objective...an order.

When you focus on non-job-related activities, you send a different message. They now are not sure of the motivation behind what you are doing.

Are your expressions of kindness, thoughtfulness, generosity, and concern a product of financial greed, or is it because you care about them as a human being. Your behavior, not your rhetoric, will make the statement for you. Individuals will always find a way to do business with someone they like.

Friendship transcends many boundaries. If your customer is your friend, everything that is important to them is of concern to you. What have you done to reflect your attitude? Did you send them a get well card when they were sick? A birthday wish? A post card when you were on vacation? Did you help a friend of theirs get an interview? Did you save that article on Little League baseball for their son? Have you had them to your home? Did you buy that silver spoon in England for their wife's collection? When was the last time you brought their cherished golden retriever something? When they told you they were going to the Caribbean on vacation, did you get them some sunscreen? Were you as readily available during their last crisis as you were when their last order was up for grabs?

As you can see, there is nothing particularly profound or complex in developing strong, long-lasting business relationships. Much of it is a matter of focus. Is yours inward or outward?

Who is more important, you or your customer? Like any successful marriage, if the partnership is a friendship, both parties are giving far more than they are taking. When the columns of activity are totaled, and the bottom line is determined, each individual made out just fine.

Over the years, I've spent time with John Clifford, and have gotten to observe his selling style up close and personal, with me and with others. Although there are variations in behavior among individuals (people are different), the fundamentals never vary.

We don't need forty adjectives to describe his actions when one will do. John Clifford, like any great Accelerator, makes his customers feel special. They feel cared about and respected. They believe their best interests are in the forefront of his thoughts. They know he likes them because he expresses it in hundreds of different ways. They are rewarded in some way for what they give to the relationship.

Do you like to drive a Mercedes? Take his for the weekend. Are you a fisherman? He will have his yacht pick you up at the dock. How about a weekend at his ocean estate? Did your daughter break her leg? He'll wait with you in the emergency room.

Does John put a lot of time and effort into selling?

Yes! But he would tell you there is no better place to spend his life than with his customers, his friends. He does so knowing the pay back will be tenfold. I am not sure when the phone call will come. I know it will; I'm just hoping he won't ask for my first born. I'd have to say yes.

Do I know that oftentimes, even though we are friends, I am being sold. I will be expected to give something back. Of course I do! But so what. In living life, I am always going to have to give something to somebody, why not give it to someone I like and respect. Let the bums go hungry!

WHEN SMOKE GETS IN YOUR EYES

A principle component of Motivational Acceleration is speed. Getting to the heart of issues is imperative if you are going to close sales rapidly. Identifying what penetrates the "Threshold of Significance" is critical. In every relationship, a sea of extraneous nonsense surrounds what is important to you and your customer. Cutting through it is a must. I've found through experience that there aren't ten issues that will determine sales success; usually it's no more than two.

As with throwing darts, you get the big score when you hit the bull's-eye. Being able to see the bull's-eye helps. When you personalize relationships, your customer will be more open and honest. They, in fact, may be incapable of giving you an order, but every customer can give you something...straight talk. In doing so, they save you time. If the sale is not to be and they let you know it, the time you would have futilely spent on them can be spent elsewhere.

When you don't personalize relationships, you are just another salesman. There is no need for special consideration. If misrepresentation, deceit, and false encouragement are part of the customer's MO, you will be a target.

I've known many salesmen who have worked years on a customer, and from day one they never had a chance. The bull's-eye wasn't visible because it was surrounded by a smoke screen. Smoke is deadly! It almost always gets you before the fire.

Personalize relationships, and you still may not get the order, but you can throw away your gas mask.

NOTES

Just our way of saying thank you.

SANTA ALWAYS HAS A PLACE AT THE TABLE

It's not what you give that's important,
it's the fact you are giving.
— Patty Pecora

The last time you went to dinner with friends and the bill came, did you divide it equally among participants, or did someone at the table convince the group that each person should pay for exactly what they consumed, right down to the peach cobbler?

As you dissected the check and allocated financial responsibility to each party, what thoughts went through your mind? What impression did that person who made the suggestion make on you: generous, successful, "big time," or unsuccessful, cheap, and "small time?"

Maybe no such perceptions were created. Friends have a way of overlooking other friends shortcomings. Friends will, but customers won't. Your customer is the key to your financial success, and I can assure you they know exactly what they have given and what they have received in return. It may not be logged in a journal, but it is indelibly etched in their mind. They know the score!

One of the best ways to show your appreciation for what they give you is through acts of generosity. Giving something back is smart selling for a number of reasons:

⇨ It shows you understand the give and take of relationships. I've found most people want a relationship that is reasonably balanced.

⇨ You create a perception of success. Who doesn't want to be around a successful person? What other successes of yours can they share in?

⇨ It creates a subliminal indebtedness. They will want to counter it with their own act of generosity.

If you haven't figured it out yet, giving to others is an emotionally rewarding way to go through life. My experience is that a majority of the successful people around are Givers. Our society is built on people giving to people. I've also come to the conclusion that selfish and cheap are an anathema to a successful relationship. I can turn to Hollywood to support my case.

"It's a Wonderful Life," a timeless Christmas classic about giving, generates tears and cheers while "Wall Street," a short-lived film about greed, has already been forgotten. Santa Claus is our hero, while Scrooge generates feelings of disdain.

I found out by accident how important it is for others to give to someone who has given something to them. My acts of generosity growing up had no basis in financial gain. For some unknown reason, I was given a Santa Claus gene. I couldn't control myself from giving what I had to others. The interesting thing was, as I gave, I received. At the time, I didn't understand the human dynamic that governs such action; I just accepted it.

As a Motivational Accelerator, I have to believe you want the most from life. Understand this! The more you give to your customers, the more they will give back. There will be periodic exceptions, and when you encounter them, adjust. In a majority of your professional and personal relationships, generosity will be rewarded. The corn will pop.

Ralph Herrmanns

In 1976, I decided to take my Army leave in Haiti. I had checked into the Hotel Olafson in Port-au-Prince, and as I walked to my room, a gentleman passed by me who appeared to be in pain. I had some aspirin with codeine leftover from a back injury, so when I saw him at the pool, I offered it. He accepted, and in gratitude, extended a dinner invitation.

It turned out the gentleman happened to be Ralph Herrmanns, one of Sweden's literary elite, and a world renowned figure. His trip to Haiti centered around doing a television documentary. In short, he was so moved by the generosity of a stranger, he invited me to tour the country in a limousine the Haitian government provided. The four days I spent with Ralph started a relationship that has lasted to this day. A small act of kindness for someone I didn't know opened a world to me that I had only read about in books. His residence and associations in Sweden are now at my disposal.

As a humorous gesture, he has found a way to insert the name Steve Sullivan in twenty of his literary works. Periodically, they are hand delivered to me in New York by one of a number of Swedish luminaries, including industrialists, prominent Swedish sculptors, artists, and politicians.

Friends of mine have been entertained by Ralph in Stockholm, and used his connections in Sweden to develop their business relationships. It is a lifetime friendship that started with $4 worth of medication.

Sam and Vicki Sebastiani

In the world of wine, Sam and Vicki Sebastiani are recognized as two of the wine industry's most dynamic people. On a flight to Europe a number of years ago I read an article about their departure from the family wine business, and how they were in the process of starting their own winery, Viansa.

The article so impressed me that I sent them both a few Osoli products with a note that said, "Good luck!" They responded quickly and I had an invitation to visit their winery!

In the interim, I continued to read about the incredible environment they were creating at Viansa. I sent them a congratulatory note and a few Osoli T-shirts. They sent back a case of wine.

Three weeks later Osoli showed up on Lifestyles of the Rich and Famous when Jon Sebastiani wore a T-shirt during the Viansa segment. I visited the winery shortly thereafter and received royal treatment.

The past two summers our families have vacationed together and the friendship is growing. My wine cabinet is filled with some of the finest wine in the world, Viansa, and I paid nothing for it. Can I put a price on the last four years of hanging around with Sam and Vicki? No, but I do know the start-up cost was $62.75.

Bruce Killen

If you don't own a work of art by Bruce Killen, I can understand why. As one of the world's top bronze sculptors, Bruce's masterpieces are very expensive.

Three years ago I was in the Medford, Oregon, airport, waiting to fly home after a Rogue River white water trip, and noticed a number of his pieces displayed in a wildlife gallery there. They were magnificent in their detail and lifelike characteristics. A promotional piece stated Bruce lived in Medford.

I had three hours to kill so I checked the phone book for his number. I wanted to call and tell him how much I appreciated his work. Everyone likes compliments. He answered and said he lived on a mountaintop just minutes from the airport. An invitation was extended to visit his studio. I jumped in my car and a short time later I stood at his front door. The following two hours were as educationally rewarding as any I have spent. I learned about sculpting and Bruce Killen. I appreciated the time he took out of a busy day to spend with me.

Bruce knew about selling. As any Accelerator knows, give and you shall receive. On the flight back to New York I thought about what Bruce had done for me and wanted to reciprocate. I bought two bronzes. With my check I sent a couple of Osoli caps as a token of appreciation for the education. He called to thank me and asked if I still liked the stainless steel, one of a kind, eagle's head I had inquired about. I said I loved it, but I didn't have $10,000 laying around to buy it. He commented he would let me have it at his foundry cost, a savings of $8,000. Two caps equaled $8,000?

The money meant nothing. The only factor in the equation involved giving. He gave...I gave...he gave...and now I own nine Bruce Killen sculptures. Who was a better salesman? Who cares.

The following summer Bruce asked me to accompany Larry Hagman, Peter Fonda, and him on a ride to Sturgis, South Dakota for the annual Harley Davidson get-together. I regrettably declined because drinking beer with Bruce Killen, J.R., and the Easy Rider would have been just too much!

Ken Noland

Amy Pecora functioned as the national sales promotion manager of Arjo Wiggins, a European manufacturer of fine art paper. One night, at dinner with her, in the course of the conversation she relayed a story to me about Ken Noland, an internationally acclaimed artist, whose pieces sell for millions. What transpired between Amy and Ken was a surprise to her, but not to me.

She had been an admirer of his work and decided as a small gesture of appreciation, to send him twenty-five sheets of watercolor paper. The cost to Amy was $75. As a way of thanking her, Ken created an original work of art on one of his posters and signed it. A gallery appraised it for several thousand dollars. Did seventy-five dollars return five thousand? No! One generous act returned another.

Motivational Accelerators understand the dynamics perfectly. They also know how to give to make the greatest impact.

    ⇨ They give unconditionally.

    ⇨ They time the delivery of the gift.

    ⇨ They down play it's worth.

    ⇨ They separate themselves from the act of giving and a desire to receive.

Decelerators do just the opposite.

    ⇨ They create an impression there are strings attached.

    ⇨ They give shortly before they are about to receive.

    ⇨ They emphasize the value of the gift not realizing the receiver will determine its worth.

    ⇨ What they give is a small fraction of what they are capable of giving.

Many unsuccessful people don't have a clue that before receiving, giving gets the Acceleration started. They think something should be given to them before they reciprocate. They fear their generosity will go unnoticed; their resources squandered. They are wrong! Just ask the Japanese. Their society is built around the act of gift giving.

Shortly after starting Osoli, we were selling a fair amount of merchandise in Japan. One of our products, the Osoli sport cap, is elaborately packaged. It comes in its own very decorative box. The importer told us the reason he thought it was a hit had very little to do with its exceptional quality. Many people bought it because it resembled a gift, waiting to be given.

Do the Japanese know what they are doing? Is gift giving part of their business success? If you don't think so, try building a relationship with a Japanese executive without giving gifts. Instead of a limousine picking you up at the airport, you'll find yourself hitchhiking.

If you choose not to be generous for the added dimension it gives to your life, do it for survival!

Beware – A generous competitor will eat you alive!!

When you are down to your last nickel, don't spend it. Give it away and it will probably return as a quarter.

Bravo, Maher. I couldn't have done it without you.

LET SOMEONE ELSE CARRY YOUR WATER

The defect of equality is we desire
it only with our superiors.
— Paul Stecko

I cannot imagine existing in a world in which I was not surrounded by friends. When I started my business career as a sales representative for International Paper, I was given a lot of input as to the negatives that surrounded a sales job. It was said that if the customers didn't get you, loneliness would. I was frightened! I had experienced it on a mountain top in Korea, one winter's night, and it was the pits. I decided then and there loneliness was not for me.

Is loneliness out there lurking in a dark alley,

waiting to make me its next victim? No way! Not if you are a Motivational Accelerator. Understand, it's not any more difficult to build a friendship across the country than across the street. There is no law that states friends need to share the same paperboy.

As I reflected back on all the great salesmen I've known, a common thread ran through the fabric of their individual selling style. No, it is not creativity, intelligence, sense of urgency, or communication skills. What they share with each other is an ability to build a successful network, a group of individuals whom they motivate to support and sustain their efforts. They recognize they are not an island unto themselves. They realize no matter how great their individual talent, it pales in comparison to a supporting cast.

MAs understand, as they achieve success, that their world will grow. Their span of control will widen. They will have to rely on others. Building a network can be one of the most important as well as personally satisfying things you do. It's critical because without a network, your success will be limited. It is emotionally satisfying because it involves expanding your association with others. An added bonus is it's easy to accomplish.

The need is obvious. A sale is not final until the customer has received what they asked for, paid their bill, and given you another order. It sounds a little geometric to me. Yes, the path any successful salesman takes is circular. The process is ongoing.

Buyers are called upon over and over again. Few salesmen could survive if they did not have a continuation of existing business. Analyze any sales transaction and you will quickly identify that a number of individuals are involved.

If we drew an analogy that selling is akin to putting a puzzle together, we would not attempt to do it unless we were sure we had all the pieces. Without each piece in place the puzzle is incomplete. From individuals at the account, to individuals in your organization, to others that hang on the periphery, anyone can make or break a sale. A MA develops and motivates his supporting cast to perform at the highest possible level whenever their interests are at stake.

They understand that the more people they have on their side, the greater the probability of success. They work on strengthening all their relationships and when they no longer call on strangers, they sell in an environment of friends. Selling becomes much like visiting family. It's comfortable. Their sales are up, complaints are down, and they are the focal point of attention whenever they make a sales call. Does any of this happen by accident? Not very often. The network needs to be nourished and rewarded. There is a basic behavioral characteristic in all of us to choose sides. We tend to support people who support us.

Methods of recognition can vary. Whether it's a letter of commendation, a pat on the back, a book, a post card, a bottle of wine, a bag of cookies, or a hundred other acts, your thoughtfulness will go a long way. It will tell them their efforts have not gone unnoticed or unappreciated, and in return, you will continue to receive favorable consideration. You will spread the word. They will pick up the ball when you drop it. View everyone as a resource and your load will be lightened.

Never underestimate the ability of anyone to perform on your behalf.

$100 Returned $10,000,000

Larry Leary is one of the best builders in Connecticut, and his commitment to quality, innovation, and giving his customers unsurpassed value, made him a home buyer's dream come true. Who wouldn't want a Leary house?

You see, even though Larry had been telling realtors and prospective clients he built great houses, nobody believed him. He had no track record. He had the reputation as the "home addition" guy, and even though his workmanship was everywhere, you couldn't find a Larry Leary house. In 1990, I met Larry, and something about him made me believe he had the ability to build a great home. I contracted to have a house built.

Larry wouldn't have labeled himself a salesman, but he knew the principles. He understood the use of Accelerators and Positive Impactors. Whatever standard we agreed upon, he quickly ignored. He upgraded everything. He didn't care if he made a profit because he recognized this opportunity would   make a statement about him. My house would be a monument to Larry's ability to perform. The relationship became symbiotic right from the start. Larry needed my money and I needed his skill.

At the first opportunity, approximately a month into the project, Larry told me, instead of a wooden deck, he thought a raised flagstone patio would look better. The cost differential happened to be substantial but he would absorb it. His input accelerated me and I wanted to encourage him to continue to make those kinds of changes. A week later, I purchased two round-trip tickets to Puerto Vallarta with his name on them and gave him the use of my condominium there for a week.

A nice house quickly turned into an estate. Larry lived up to every expectation. He went from builder to friend and because of that I decided I would save the best for last. Upon completion of the house, I would make Larry the most sought after builder in the state. It wouldn't be difficult because I understood the value of testimonials; input given by someone else. For some reason, when another individual delivers the message, it becomes more credible, less biased, and of greater worth. I would testify for Larry Leary.

He completed the job and the house was terrific. I told Larry so, and he was happy to hear it, but that did nothing for his bank account. Ten minutes of my time and $100 did. As a matter of fact, he went from Larry ? to celebrity status overnight. Yes, I said it, overnight. Rather than keeping my feelings to myself, I decided to share them with the community. Because I wanted to accelerate the process, the dinner party circuit wouldn't do, too slow and too fattening. I evaluated a number of possible Positive Impactors, and made my choice. A week later, a half-page ad appeared in the local paper. It read, "Thanks Larry Leary Construction Management for a terrific house and a wonderful building experience – The Sullivans." His phone started ringing that day and hasn't stopped.

Getting things accomplished doesn't necessarily take hard work. It often depends on just knowing how the game is played.

Hardly a month goes by when I'm not contacted by an executive headhunter, looking to put me into a job somewhere in corporate America. The call never changes in the introductory phase. "I've been given your name by someone who tells me you're the perfect candidate for this opportunity." They know nothing about me, but because another person said I was okay, I'm okay. Had I called them and suggested I was okay, they probably would have hung up. Second-party communication is the foundation of the advertising business. Apple Computers are not okay until Burnes Hollyman says they're okay.

MAs are others centered. They find great satisfaction in sharing their success and recognition. They institutionalize the process of acknowledging everyone's accomplishment. They treat others as they would want to be treated. Their objective is to make their supporters feel like winners, and in doing so, it becomes a self-fulfilling prophecy. They will act as winners.

The entire process is self-perpetuating, and the payment for your effort is success!!

I told you I thought he was a vegetarian!

IT STARTED
WITH CAVEMEN

Everyone lives by selling something.
— *Robert Louis Stevenson*

If I were asked to come up with a list of adjectives that accurately described a Motivational Accelerator, it would probably fill a page. If I were limited to just one synonym, it would be communicator.

Everything a salesman does is for naught if it cannot be communicated to the Buyer. The history books are filled with examples of people and organizations who failed for only one reason; they didn't understand how important it was to get the message out.

The lessons learned are a matter of record, so I'm amazed at how poorly many salesmen express themselves, verbally and in writing. It's apparent they have no concept of the perception they create when their communication skills are lacking. There is a direct correlation between one's ability to express oneself and success. If you are unable to get knowledge from your brain past your lips, your climb up the ladder of success will approximate an assault on Mt. Everest.

Salesmen are paid to communicate! If you can't your worth is marginal! Over the years, I've had the misfortune of listening to a countless number of sales presentations that were ill prepared, poorly given, and extremely boring. Within minutes after the salesman started, my thoughts took flight to a South Pacific island. When the sales pitch was finished, and I was asked for the order, because I had not been mentally present there was nothing I could say but no! The salesman obviously didn't comprehend if my mind wasn't into it, my wallet wouldn't be either.

For the want of a nail the shoe was lost - Ben Franklin.

There are hundreds of activities that surround the process of getting something sold. If 99% of them are accomplished, and the salesman lets the communication link break, nothing happens. Everyone's efforts are wasted.

Being able to articulate your thoughts clearly is critical. It's one of my hot buttons. Anyone who works for me will have to become an excellent communicator, and it is a prerequisite for long-term employment. I'm doing them a favor by forcing the issue.

My name is Ma – Ma – Ma – Maurie.

I recognize a lot of individuals shy away from public speaking. Research has discovered it is the #1 fear people have. I would have thought being locked in a cage with twenty pit bulls with rabies would be more frightening, but I guess not.

THE PROBLEM

If you are afraid of public speaking, you will avoid opportunities to do it, and in so doing, you will shortchange yourself and your company.

The message needs to get out and the salesman must play the role of messenger.

THE OPPORTUNITY

In recognizing the need to become a better communicator, you will work on it. Practice makes perfect. As your abilities grow, your confidence will also. You'll become a walking presentation. It won't take long to realize it's as easy to address an audience of one hundred as it is one, and it's certainly more productive.

As you perform, you become a much more valuable asset. In addition, because so many salesmen are such poor communicators, you will stand out. Your customers will recognize your ability and see you as a resource they can use. You will be asked to help them deliver their message. Now you're part of their network. Things are heating up.

As I've said, I've given hundreds of speeches and

it's always a rewarding experience. It breaks up the routine of life. I never know when a plane ticket will land on my desk with an invitation to join a group in Jackson Hole, Miami or Brussels. All I have to bring is a few thoughts. The rest is on them.

If you haven't figured it out yet, building a vocabulary pays a lot more than building a bicep.

Jim Fleming

I remember Jim when he thought a big night on the town meant dinner at Denny's. He's come a long way. As executive vice president of UNISOURCE, the world's largest paper distribution network, he is the epitome of a great communicator. Not only does he understand the importance of keeping everyone informed, he does it with such linguistic aplomb that people marvel at his ability to express himself. Listen to Jim deliver a presentation and you are convinced he knows everything. His message is so perspicuous, you now know everything. Is it an accident he's been promoted twenty times (slight exaggeration) in ten years, or does the fact he taught Dale Carnegie how to punctuate a sentence have anything to do with it?

Motivational Accelerators understand enlightenment involves more than the information that is passed from them to their audience. Great communication involves managing the process. In order to do that, you need an understanding of a critical component...

THE GRAPEVINE

Are you thinking about Napa Valley? Don't! The grapevine I'm talking about has nothing to do with Merlot, Chardonnay, or Cabernet grapes. Our grapevine is a vehicle through which information is passed along, in many cases at supersonic speeds.

This is the communication age! Billion dollar organizations have been created overnight by giving the consumer products that allow them to communicate more quickly. Who wants to wait an hour to make contact when you can pull a phone out of your briefcase and do it instantaneously?

It's not a difficult deduction to understand that the quicker one can communicate, the more one will communicate. Look around you. We are bombarded by information. Everywhere! Twenty-four hours a day, seven days a week, 365 days a year, people are talking to us, about us. Much of it is "noise," and the delivery mechanisms, in many cases, are inane, but we are listening! Not only do we listen, but we pass along much of what we hear.

MAs understand how important a communication network is to their success. They want as many people to know about them as possible. They recognize any individual effort in promoting themselves or their product can't compare to the collective effort of a support group. Get lots of people saying nice things about you. Let them express favorable opinions and accelerate the process.

There is something about input coming from others that appears less self-serving. Tell people you're great and they'll think you're egotistical. Let someone else deliver the message, and it becomes a truth.

MAs know how to get the word out. They use the grapevine. It's easy to get the process started because there is a tendency in all of us to gossip. We love to take information in and pass it along.

You may prefer to think of yourself as a conduit of information, or a communication link. Certainly gossip is frivolous, and in your efforts to develop a productive grapevine, you want information passed along that is more substantive. Adjectives like honest, credible, adventurous, thoughtful, kind, concerned, knowledgeable, aware, creative, informed, and more can paint a picture of you that generates interest in others.

They want to meet you. They've heard you're unique, different. All of a sudden, your horizons have expanded. Opportunities are coming in from a variety of different directions. You are a professional! You can be trusted! Much of the effort to create this perception and reaction went on unbeknownst to you. Others did the work.

Once you understand what a powerful tool the grapevine is, you take all precautions to protect your image within it. Proper fertilization

(Accelerators) engender growth, while improper fertilization (Decelerators) kill. The grapes needs to be nourished, not poisoned.

MAs recognize that Decelerators move through the grapevine as quickly or quicker than Accelerators, and they guard against any destructive input. If, for some reason, negative information about you is generated, take immediate corrective action. Speed is of the essence. Flood the conduit of information with Accelerators to neutralize the Decelerator.

In the event it reaches the grapevine, it does so in a weakened state. The impact is lessened. Accelerators arrive shortly thereafter, and the damage will have been minimized. The MA recognizes the potentially disastrous effects of negative publicity, and does whatever is necessary to prevent it.

THE NON-ACCELERATOR

A Non-Accelerator's view of a grapevine is ten grapes. Ten mutant grapes whose genetic makeup did not allow for a tongue. They keep everything to themselves. Abuse them, lie to them, ignore them; it doesn't matter, they can't talk. What happened yesterday will soon be forgotten and forgiven. No one else will know. Or will they? Wait a second, ten people know ten people. That's a hundred. Yes, the grapevine can make or break you. It has an insatiable appetite. Make sure you become its dietitian.

The Grapevine
Non-Accelerator's View

The Grapevine
Accelerator's View

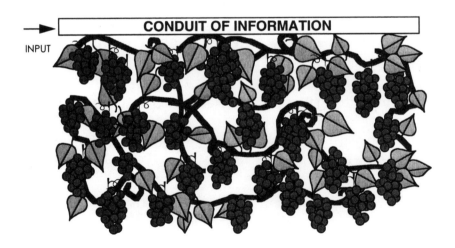

Tim Needham

If you haven't been to the War Room in the Pentagon, and wonder what that experience is all about, don't call Colin Powell, call Tim Needham, president of Williamhouse-Regency Inc. The activity level is about the same. Both men know that to win any war, intelligence is a critical component for success. I have not met an individual in my military, business, or personal life that has a better understanding or operational capability, when it comes to The Grapevine than Needham.

Sit in his office for twenty minutes, and you will understand why AT&T has voted him customer of the year, ten years running. The phone never stops ringing, and Tim never stops calling. Information is received analyzed, and dispatched to its proper place.

He is the executive equivalent of a switching device. Everything comes through him, and because of that, he sits atop a mountain of intelligence. Want to know something? Call Tim. Need to get your message out? Needham will be happy to oblige.

Success in selling involves participation, and because Tim Needham has been fertilizing grapes longer than Mike Sebastiani, he is always a player.

Notes

Whew!

A TWO–SIDED GRAVE

Do not go where the path may lead.
Go instead where there is no
path and leave a trail
— Doug Turner

One of the rewards of having knowledge about something is periodically sharing it with others. Over the years, I have been involved in countless training sessions in the area of sales and marketing. Although each group differed in a variety of ways, I have observed there is one characteristic that remained constant—their ability to be creative. That's the good news. The bad news is that creativity, too often, is only seen in an academic setting.

Academia is a warm and loving place. Nobody gets fired there, at least not the students. They know that, so they go for broke. Unfortunately, much of what is created in the classroom never makes it to the streets.

For some reason, their open-minded approach to problem solving is an idiosyncratic characteristic relegated to intellectual settings. Once their educational experience is over, and they are back on the job, their creativity takes residence in the closet under lock and key. They crawl back into the same Non-Eventful rut they were in before, and go merrily, or not so merrily, on their way. Why? My guess is it has something to do with laziness or fear of failure. Laziness, because it's easier to do things the way they've always been done. No brain power needed. Just reach into that old bag of tricks and pull something out. No matter, the customer has seen the trick a dozen times.

Fear? Understandable! Nobody likes to fail.

But what a mediocre salesman doesn't understand, and a MA does, is that the use of creativity in energizing relationships is not hard work; it's fun work. Exploring different ways to do things often results in uncovering new and better ways to do things. In the process of energizing your customer, you will energize yourself. Boredom will take flight.

You might say your unwillingness to be creative has nothing to do with being lazy; you just don't want to fail. I applaud your concern. Show me a person who doesn't mind failing and...!!

The opportunities to fail in life are everywhere. Well, that's not exactly correct. There is no chance of failing when being creative with a customer.

Successful selling involves your ability to differentiate yourself from your competition. If you can't, you are running with the herd and that's a Non-Event.

Creativity will enable you to stand out. Look around you, the people and businesses that are succeeding are breaking the mold. Who says cappuccino doesn't sell in bookstores, rickshaws can't transport people in Coconut Grove, and you can't order a leather jacket with your hamburger? Bring a little ingenuity into your customer's world, and even if you don't solve the problem, you'll score big when it comes to setting yourself apart.

I mentioned earlier that I've given a lot of speeches and I'm under no misconception as to why I'm in demand. I'm the only professional speaker in America that speaks for free. (I guess that makes me an amateur.) In addition, my presentations get pretty wild. I've found people like craziness. They always stay awake. The message gets heard.

Creativity doesn't necessitate playing an accordion while giving the features, advantages, and benefits of your service in Swahili. It does mean coming up with stimulating alternatives to what is presently being done. If you are doing the same things as your competition...you lose.

Use your competitor as a benchmark for your actions. If they bring donuts, counter with corn dogs. I've found creative people take a simple act and make it an event by modifying it in some way. (The Accelerators in Chapter 3 are just a start.) If you don't happen to be the creative type, use your network. Find someone who can assist you. Help is everywhere. Call me!

WHO WAS THAT MAN ON THE WATER BUFFALO

Eric Weber, a highly successful businessman in upstate New York, became a legend by turning vacation photos into post cards and then sending them to his customers. The photos are so absurd and humorous people can't wait for the next one to arrive. Needless to say, Eric is always in their thoughts. The card arrives, the corn pops, and Eric becomes a little wealthier.

As an MA, you don't need to reinvent the wheel. Creative solutions are everywhere. If you can't identify them, rip someone else off. What matters is not where the creativity came from; what's important is that it showed up. A good joke is told ten million times. What works in Burma may work in Mississippi. The world is becoming smaller and you have almost instant access to it.

One of the most creative individuals I associate with these days is my vice president of sales. He wasn't always that way. I just had to get his snow-ball rolling. Once upon a time he was an empiricist. He loved numbers. Since he's been in sales, he now recognizes the need to make two plus two equal eight.

HARTFORD. DRY RIBS? JOHN GRYMES!

I remember the sales call vividly. I functioned as national sales manager at International Paper Company, and accompanied John Grymes, the sales representative, who had account responsibility for a very tough, unyielding buyer in Hartford. It just so happened that the buyer went to school in Memphis, where IP was headquartered. Memphis is known for many things, none more important than Elvis and dry ribs from the Rendezvous.

The buyer, after telling us we still would not get the business, started to discuss what he missed most about Memphis. Surprisingly, the ribs took precedent over Elvis. Thirty seconds later John excused himself from the table and went to a pay phone. The call to the Rendezvous placed an order for ribs to be air expressed to Hartford. The note inside said, "Thanks for taking time to hear our story. Your friends at IP." Yes, shortly thereafter, IP got the business. Without getting into any psychological analysis, here's what I think transpired.

The buyer, even though he said we wouldn't get the business, hadn't made up his mind. Buyers have been known to misrepresent the facts on occasion. In reality, he had been energized by John on previous calls and found himself close to Acceleration. Two Accelerators, or one Impactor would do it.

Only a creative person would recognize the death of a cow in Tennessee could lead to the birth of a relationship in Connecticut. John is a MA but his choice of Impactor was not "Rocket Science." The customer had identified something of importance to them and John acted on it, immediately.

It's not surprising when you give customers what they desire quickly, and do it in a way that is different, very often they will give something in return...an order.

I'll conclude my thoughts on creativity by being blunt. Get a new bag of tricks! Whatever the added cost, your customer will probably make up the difference by giving you a better lifestyle.

Notes

Derouin, I told you not to ask for the order!

STAND YOUR GROUND

To know what is right and not to
do it is the worst cowardice.
— Kenneth Branch

W hen I reflect back on my twenty years of professional selling, and attempt to identify what behavioral characteristics made the greatest impression on my customers, four come to mind:

➊ Kindness

➋ Commitment

➌ Generosity

➍ Courage

There is probably room for debate as to the level of emotional impact any of these actions engendered in a buyer, with one exception, **Courage**.

America is a society built around the concept that standing up for what you believe in separates the winners from the losers. It's the stuff of legends and great books. I don't know of anyone who read, "A Milk Toast For All Seasons."

In the world markets, backbone is traded as a precious commodity. It provides a foundation on which to build a relationship. Motivationally Accelerated Selling requires a lot of courage. MAs recognize the more times they take action, the greater the opportunity for success, but also failure. They operate outside the Comfort Zone because they know in selling, batting average means nothing!

Making two hundred calls, and closing on fifty is far better than making ten with five of them being a success. They do not let the fear of rejection inhibit their ability to act.

MAs recognize rejection is not an indictment about their worth to the human race. It's merely a puddle in the road on their journey to enlightenment and future success. How many times was Lord Laurence Olivier rejected before he became an icon...after he became one?

When you are rejected, read between the lines. I seriously doubt the message is "I hate you;" it probably reads more like, "Not at this time."

Have you Decelerated lately? Is your customer waiting for three more Accelerators and a Positive Impactor. Evaluate your situation. Make whatever corrections are necessary and attack again.

You'll find there are a plethora of buyers who reject for rejection's sake. They want to see what your counter will be. Have you ever heard about the path of least resistance?

I know of no one who wants a relationship with a coward! The proverbial "tail between your legs" doesn't illicit sympathy. It generates disgust.

John Wayne stood his ground!

MAs operate under no misconception as to the traffic patterns in a relationship. There are no one-way streets. The nature of successful partnerships dictates as you give, you shall receive. The concept is the cornerstone of any business. Your buyer expects to receive from their customers, and for them to think you should accept less is hypocrisy. Do not allow it to occur!

Your time and energy has value. The second a buyer accepts your service, they have established a contract with you. The fact it is not a written contract makes no difference. What does matter is you live up to your end of the agreement so the buyers will live up to theirs.

If you do, you have earned a right to a portion of their business. If you are not getting it, it might be due to lethargy or ignorance on the buyer's part. They may be unaware of all that you have done. Educate them!

There is a cost associated with selling, and it must be covered. There is no risk in asking for the order. I cannot remember anyone trying to kill me for saying, "I want some of the business." In most cases, I received what I asked for, but when I didn't, I was no worse off than before I made the request. My ego may have been bruised, but I recovered. When you compare the risk associated with selling with that of other professions: police work, firefighting, or the military, it pales by comparison.

Why not let it all hang out? A turtle goes nowhere until it sticks its neck out. I suspect the same happens with salesmen.

There is only one absolute truth in selling: you are responsible for your actions. If you are willing to put forth the effort, success is guaranteed. With that success comes more than financial gain. As a Motivational Accelerator, you will receive the respect of the individuals you work with as well as the customers you sell.

Life will become very, very good!

Notes

·No Sale·

·Sale·

LAVRICELLA

You reap what you sow.

THE FINAL
WORD

Today is not the first day of the rest of your life.
It's all there is of your life.
— Douglas Byther

What you have read throughout the previous chapters is one man's view on selling. My knowledge of the subject did not come from a vision. It has evolved over the past two decades; from speeches I've given, individuals I've trained and managed, buyers that have said yes, and those that said no.

Through all of it, one undeniable truth comes out. Salesmen who have the greatest success, those that Sell at Mach 1, recognize the customer is not a sideshow. They brought the circus to town. They understand to view it any other way engenders actions that shortchange the relationship. When their time is no longer your time, and requests for help are acted upon slowly, when what they give to make you a success is treated with callous indifference you're in trouble.

Over the years I have seen salesmen that would have been ideal for the cover of the Dale Carnegie Digest, but couldn't sell lemonade in the Mojave Desert. Physically they had it all, but somewhere in their sales orientation they developed an attitude that the customer was nothing more than a necessary nuisance. Because of that, their success was a fraction of what it could have been.

In contrast, I've seen superstars who had no formal selling education, appeared disheveled, and presented their case with the sophistication of a jackhammer operator. Somehow they were still Masters of the Universe. Everyone wanted to give them an order. Why? I've told you why. Believe it!

Certainly there is more to being successful than giving your customer a box of Valentine's Day chocolates. Professionalism is part of the equation. Sales training is important in fine-tuning your selling techniques. If you haven't had any, get some, but recognize knowing what to do and how to do it is worthless if a program of customer directed activities doesn't follow. If it does, get ready to leave a vapor trail.

FROM HERE TO WHERE

Over the past 167 pages you've been given my thoughts on how to have greater success in selling.

In the course of developing the concepts and putting them on paper, I have thought through the issues a number of times and for me, now, it all seems pretty simple.

You in contrast, have been exposed to Motivational Acceleration for a period no longer than the time it took you to read the book. I would hope it makes sense to you and if I were more naive in my view of what it takes to motivate people to act on something, I'd believe you would start Accelerating today.

Reality dictates that trying new and different approaches is not easy for most of us and unless a degree of confidence can be created that a program of change will work, nothing transpires.

My ego won't allow that to happen. I don't want to go into your memory bank as the author who entertained you for five hours. I want status as the guy who helped you become a sales superstar.

It's a complex world we live in, but not everything we do needs to be complex. In many situations the correct solution to the problem involves simplifying the procedures that address the issue. In the world of high technology it's called "reengineering."

In government bureaucracy, the more successful managers recognize that programs introduced a decade ago may no longer be appropriate for what is happening today. A process called "zero-based budgeting" mandates allocation of resources must be justified anew.

Whatever the environment, future success for

any organization or individual will parallel their ability to adapt to change! The process starts with an evaluation. Whether it's daily, monthly, or yearly, you need to objectively measure where you are in your customer relationships. Call it a customer audit. Let them give you a report card on your performance. It can be as easy as calling them and asking where you can improve. Pay less attention to what they say than the enthusiasm in which they say it. If the news is good, it will establish a level of performance on which to build, and if it is bad, view it as a cathartic exposé and adjust your behavior immediately.

Here is your action plan and it starts with the five questions: Who? What? When? Where? Why? and How?

WHO: Start small! You may have a population of a hundred buyers you want to Accelerate, but the first thing you need to do is build some confidence that Motivational Acceleration works. The process takes energy and commitment. All of which are given with the intent of getting a return on your investment.

Identify five of the most important people you want to sell and start with them. In working with a smaller body of individuals you can better concentrate your efforts while reducing your resource exposure. As they respond to your efforts your belief in the process will grow and you'll be ready for a quantum leap forward.

WHAT: Start with a thank-you letter. There is

always a reason to thank someone for something. When communication comes unexpectedly it usually carries substantial impact. Remember, I said start with five of your most important customers. You can thank them for the relationship, their time, consideration, or a myriad of other things. If you have been doing a great job for them the thank-you will be just one more Accelerator that scores points.

If your efforts have been marginal up to that point, the thank-you will have the effect of a cleansing agent. It will establish a reference point from which to Accelerate. Whatever you did prior to that can be forgotten if everything that follows is customer directed. Whatever else you decide to do after the thank-you is up to you.

WHEN: Intuition plays a large part in timing. My suggestion is sooner is always better than later. At any given point in time your customer may be on the verge of making a decision that will favor you or your competition. It's important your actions be viewed with a certain naturalness, but if you aren't sure whether to do something now or in the future, do it now. Two of the most frustrating words in the English language are "what if." Taking action eliminates them.

WHERE: Trying to decide "where" starts with evaluating your alternatives. Environment plays a large part in the significance of any action. As best you can, try to isolate your customers so they receive the full impact of what you are doing. Getting them away from their place of business and all the irritants that go with it can make a major difference in how your message is received.

Contact your best customer, immediately, and invite them to a place that you know they like and therefore, will be receptive to your invitation. Between their acceptance and the actual date, you have plenty of time to come up with numerous Accelerators and Impactors that will make a statement: they are special and you are different.

WHY: Experience is a wonderful teacher! As you experiment with different approaches, you will learn what works and what doesn't. Wasted effort will be minimized and every well-executed action will score.

HOW: Let me give you three things to consider before starting your Motivational Acceleration program.

❶ Don't try to close too quickly!

In most things there is a warm-up period, an introductory phase. You have to get through it before you can Accelerate. If you can't get out of the starting blocks, you'll never cross the finish line. Your customer was doing business long before you arrived on the scene. Although you are full of enthusiasm and desire to do the deal, much of what you will tell them has been heard before! Your consistent performance over time will determine the success of the relationship. Corn does not pop in two-and-a-half minutes.

❷ Most success is not characterized by
a quantum leap forward; it manifests
itself incrementally.

Every journey begins with an initial step. Identify
what you feel most comfortable with and start
there. As you achieve success and fine-tune your
approach, you can take bigger strides.

❸ The two most important numbers in
selling are eighty and twenty.

Anyone who has been a salesman for any period
of time recognizes that a majority of their success
comes from a minority of their accounts (80/20).
Your time, energy, and resources are finite. Identify
where you appear to have the greatest opportunity
for success, and concentrate a major portion of your
effort there. Treat everyone like you would want to
be treated, but treat some better than others. In reality, customers exist who are not worthy of your
Motivationally Accelerated efforts, and therefore
should not receive them.

I now think you have enough to get started, but
let me make one final suggestion. Buy a full length
mirror, and put it next to where you exit your residence. Each day, as you leave to take on the world,
you might as well see how you are seen.

THE PROOF IS IN THE PUDDING

What follows is not a unique case. It is happening
everywhere. I relay it only because I have watched

it evolve over the past ten years.

John Papa started his career as a salesman at International Paper Company. Well, at least John knew he had sales capability. The title on his business card said mailboy.

He delivered newspapers and mail, and he did it with such enthusiasm you thought you had received the Declaration of Independence. (He stood out.) It didn't take long for John to get noticed and promoted to the cashier's window. As usual, John took a mundane activity and turned it into an event.

Did I want to lunch with Malcolm Forbes or experience the thrill of having John Papa cash my check. (He knew how to differentiate himself.)

Shortly after my first encounter with John, a position became available in the customer service group. It reported through me, and when I asked my operations manager if he had found a replacement, he stated he had a number of resumes and fifty phone calls about a guy named John Papa. (John was using his network.)

Even though he didn't carry the academic and operational qualifications, he got the job. Almost instantly he excelled. John knew who paid his salary – The Customer. Every customer request received immediate attention. He developed a reputation for speed, and they showed their appreciation with orders.

He became such a star, the president of International Paper came down from his perch to shake John's hand. We promoted him to supervisor, and within days he had instilled the same customer directed enthusiasm to his subordinates that he carried. Promoted again!

I left International Paper, and hired him into an outside sales position. Soon after, another promotion to regional sales manager followed. His customers adore him, his competitors fear him, and I suspect before John hangs up his selling spurs, he'll write enough orders to fill a garbage dump.

In my experience with John, I have yet to see a situation in which he played a part that didn't turn out to be an immediate success. It has nothing to do with how he looks or speaks. He'll never be a stand-in for Tom Cruise, and that's Queens, New York, not Cambridge, Massachusetts, in his voice.

What John possesses is the same attitude that makes any Motivational Accelerator successful. He understands the customer relationship is not a means to an end, it is **The End**.

The Author's Recommended Reading List

Bible

Bill of Rights

Boy Scout Creed

Constitution of the United States

Declaration of Independence

Gettysburg Address

Girl Scout Creed

Koran

Magna Carta

Ranger Handbook

Torah

Encyclopedia of Sales Success
Contributors: Sunny Olzman, Marty Lewis,
Norm Hamer, Ed Norton, Tony Urgola,
Lou Weintraub, Jim Coromilas, and
Marvin Cohen

About The Author

Steve Sullivan's management and sales expertise are a product of a highly diversified background. Regardless of the responsibility; Army officer, National Sales Manager at International Paper Company, Executive Vice President of Williamhouse-Regency, founder of Osoli Inc., or any of his other nine job titles, Steve has an inate ability to make things happen, quickly. His formula for success has changed very little over the past twenty-two years.

He recognizes the common thread that runs through almost every issue centers around people, so his focus is always interpersonal. When asked what he sees as the single most important skill a person needs to succeed, his reply comes as no surprise: "An ability to sell."

Selling at Mach 1 is Sullivans's highly entertaining, easily understood, and readily adaptable analysis of what all of us are trying to do: Sell.

Steve is a nationally recognized speaker on the subjects of sales, marketing, and management, and has spent two decades helping make organizations more productive. He holds a BA from the University of Florida and a Masters in Systems Management from the University of Southern California.